Let's Play Games in German

ELISABETH SCHMIDT: *Let's*

Play

Games

in

German

National Textbook Company
a division of *NTC Publishing Group* • Lincolnwood, Illinois USA

1990 Printing

Published by National Textbook Company, a division of NTC Publishing Group.
© 1987, 1977 by NTC Publishing Group, 4255 West Touhy Avenue,
Lincolnwood (Chicago), Illinois 60646-1975 U.S.A.
Manufactured in the United States of America.

0 ML 9 8 7 6 5 4 3 2

*To all my students
in Williamsburg and
in Iowa City*

Foreword

Ease and fluency in German conversation can be promoted through the use of individual or group activities. Games, by themselves, do not form the core of any course but they do serve to stimulate the student's enthusiasm and interest.

The games of this collection have a threefold purpose: to help students communicate clearly and fluently in German, to improve their facility in the language by offering a wide variety of activities requiring German responses, and to provide an enjoyable learning experience.

Let's Play Games in German is geared to grades 9 to 12, but many games are popular in the lower grades as well. The games range in difficulty, from simple to those which require more flexibility and manipulation with the language. The class or club may play these games again and again to become familiar with the vocabulary and structures, thus reinforcing important material through entertaining means.

The explanations and directions for playing the games are presented in English. The dialogue for the games is in German with an English translation. To facilitate selection, the book is organized into twelve areas of concentration—spelling, article, verb, number, word recall and construction, object identification, category, asking and answering, clue and description, map, song, and storytelling games. The aim of each game and the number of players and articles needed are declared after each title.

Elisabeth Schmidt has compiled this collection of games and activities from many that have proven to be effective aids in teaching foreign language. Another program and activity resource by the same author is *The German Club in High School,* published by National Textbook Company.

Contents

x

Spelling Games

The aim of all the games in this section is the correct spelling of German words.

1. *Baseball*

PLAYERS: The class is divided into two teams.

The game is played like baseball, only with the team at bat spelling words instead of hitting a ball. Before the game starts, each team chooses a captain, makes up a list of difficult German words which the class has had (the teacher may wish to check each list), and decides on a batting order. The first person at bat must spell correctly the word which the other team-pitcher gives him. If he does, he gets a homerun, scoring a point for his team. If he spells the word incorrectly, he's out, and the next person on the team is up at bat. If the pitcher pronounces the German word incorrectly, the player walks home and the team at bat scores a point. After three outs, the other team is up at bat.

2. *Spelldown*

PLAYERS: The class is divided into two teams.

The teacher alternates between teams in asking members to spell a German word. A team scores a point for each word its team members spell correctly. The game can be played to 21 points or according to a predetermined time limit.

3. *Funny Spelling*

PLAYERS: The class is divided into two or more teams.

Each player must spell correctly the German word the teacher gives him. Before the game starts, however, the class decides on two letters which will not be spoken but, instead, will be acted out in a particular way, as by waving a hand or stamping a foot. A point is scored for each word correctly spelled.

4. *Spelling Relay*

PLAYERS: The class is divided into two or more teams.

At a desk in front of each team is a pile of scrambled letters which spell a word. The teams compete to see which one can spell its word correctly first.

5. *Letter People*

PLAYERS: The class is divided into groups of five.

The teacher gives each person in a group a letter which contributes to the spelling of a five-letter German word. The team which arranges itself in the correct spelling of the five-letter German word first wins.

II

Article Games

6. *Der-, Die-, oder Das-Liste*   (*Der, die,* or *das* List)

AIM: To think of all the German words possible which take
           a given article.
PLAYERS: Each row works as a team.

The teacher chooses an article, *die* for example. Each row writes
down all the *die* words it can think of. At the end of two minutes, the
team with the largest number of *die* words correctly spelled in German
wins. A point is subtracted from the final score for any *der* word or
das word in the lists.

7. *Der-, Die-, Das-Bingo*   (*Der, die, das* Bingo)

AIM: To associate a German word with its correct article.
PLAYERS: The whole class.
NEEDED: Mimeographed sheets of paper containing a box
           seven squares wide and seven squares deep, and a
           blackboard.

Each student receives a mimeographed sheet of paper with 49 squares.
The square in the middle is "free" and is called *Ei-frei*. At the top of
all the remaining 48 squares each student writes either *der*, *die*, or
das. When all of the students have written an article at the top of
each square on their sheet of paper, the teacher begins to call out
German nouns. Each time the students hear a noun whose gender

3

they recall, they write this German word as quickly as possible in a box with the correct article at the top.

Because the teacher continues calling out German nouns without stopping, many students may miss several words during the course of the game, while they are writing a preceding word. But when a student has a Bingo, he rushes to the board, writes the seven German words with their articles which form his Bingo, and initials his list. He then rushes back to continue playing, in an attempt to get another Bingo.

The game is over when there are 12 Bingos on the board, or when 20 minutes are up. The teacher corrects the Bingos. If even one article is incorrect, the student receives no points for the Bingo. If all of the articles in the Bingo are correct, the student receives seven points, plus an additional point for each noun which is spelled correctly.

8. *Der-, Die-, Das-Klatsch*   (*Der, die, das* Clap)

AIM: To recall a German word which has the gender of a given article.

PLAYERS: The whole class.

Students sit in a circle. A certain rhythm of clapping is used in the game, which the students must practice before the game begins. The rhythm is four claps (one count each), followed by snapping of the right-hand fingers (two counts), and then by snapping of the left-hand fingers (two counts). The rhythm must never be broken.

When everyone has the rhythm, the leader calls out an article at the time when everyone is snapping the fingers of their left hand.

Assume that the leader calls out *die*. The rhythm continues to the finger snapping of the right hand, at which time the next person in the circle must immediately call out a feminine noun, because the article specified by the preceding player was *die*. He follows in the next two counts with any article.

Assume that this player calls out *das*. The game continues around the circle, with each succeeding player naming a noun which takes the aforementioned article (on finger snapping of the right hand) and immediately calling out an article for the next person (on finger snapping of the left hand).

III

Verb Games

The aim of the games in this section is to use German verbs in their correct forms. The games can be used to emphasize *ich* and *du* forms, *ich* and *Sie* forms, or *er* and *sie* forms.

9. *Kettenspiel* (Chain Game)

PLAYERS: The whole class.

The first person calls on a classmate and asks him a question, using the pronoun *du* and the *du* form of a verb, for example:

    Karl, malst du?   Karl, do you paint?

His neighbour replies *Ja* or *Nein*, using the pronoun *ich* and the *ich* form of the verb:

    Ja, ich male.   Yes, I paint.

He then directs a question to another person in the room and so on.

Each time a person either asks or answers a question correctly in German, he receives one point. The teacher may request the students to call on each other in the order of the seating arrangement so that everyone gets the same number of chances to participate. Similarly, questions may be asked in the *Sie* instead of the *du* form.

Also, this game may be used to practice the third person singular, as follows:

    Lore, malt Karl?   Lore, does Karl paint?

    Ja, Karl malt.   Yes, Karl paints.

> *Heidi, singt Helene?*   Heidi, does Helene sing?
> *Ja, Helene singt.*   Yes, Helene sings.
> *Klaus, kommt Werner?*   Klaus, is Werner coming?
> *Ja, Werner kommt.*   Yes, Werner is coming.

10. *Was tue ich?*   (What Am I Doing?)

PLAYERS: The class is divided into two teams.

Using familar verbs, each team (or the teacher) writes a list of commands which a student could do (or pantomime) in the classroom. Each command should be written on a separate sheet of paper. Each team then selects a captain who takes the slips of paper with commands from the opposing team and sits in front of the class with the papers turned face down. In alternating sequence, each team captain draws a slip of paper, responds to the command, and asks:

> *Was tue ich?*   What am I doing?

To score a point, his team must reply correctly with the correct *du* form of the verb, for example:

> *Du schläfst.*   You are sleeping.
> *Du schwimmst.*   You are swimming.

If the captain doesn't know the command or is mistaken in its meaning, his team must forfeit its turn. A time limit is set for each turn.

IV

Number Games

The aim of all of the games in this section is to practice counting and working with numbers in German.

11. *Welche Nummer hast du?*   (What Number Do You Have?)

PLAYERS: The whole class.
NEEDED: A ball or similar item.

The players form a circle and each one is assigned a number. The leader, in the center of the circle, calls out a number, such as *fünf* (five), and tosses a ball to the person who has that number. This person, as he catches the ball, must repeat his number. He must then call another number and toss the ball across the circle to the player who has that number. The second person repeats the action of the first player, remembering to repeat his own number before he calls the next one. The game continues in this manner.

12. *Wie oft?*   (How Often?)

PLAYERS: The whole class.
NEEDED: A large ball.

The players form a circle. One player begins by bouncing the ball as he counts: *eins, zwei, drei,* etc. When he makes a mistake, or can

7

count no further, another takes his place with the ball. Or the teacher may set a limit on the number of times each player may bounce the ball, after which he must pass it to another player, who repeats the same count.

13. **Wo ist es? eins, zwei** . . .   (Where Is It? One, Two . . .)

PLAYERS: Up to 40.
NEEDED: Any convenient object that can be hidden.

One player is sent out of the room and the others decide upon a pencil, a key, or other object to be hidden somewhere in the room. The leader goes to the door and speaks to the person who has been sent out:

Leader:
   Herein!   Come in.
Player:
   Danke schön.   Thank you.
  As the player comes in, the leader asks him where the object is:
Leader:
   Wo ist der Bleistift?   Where is the pencil?
Player:
   Ich weiss nicht.   I don't know.
Leader:
   Guck mal nach!   Look for it!

The player begins searching for the object as the group counts in unison: *Eins, zwei, drei*, etc. They count as far as they wish to go. When the player approaches the hidden article, their voices are raised. When the player goes farther away, the words are spoken softly. When the object has been found, the player holds it up before the class and says:
  Hier ist der Bleistift!   Here's the pencil!

• As a variation, the group can say the days of the week or the months of the year in unison, instead of counting.

14. *Schnapp hat den Hut verloren.*   (Schnapp Lost His Hat.)

PLAYERS: The whole class.

Everyone sits in a circle and gets a number starting with "one".

The person to the right of number one, however, doesn't have a number. He is called "Schnapp" and begins the game by saying:

Schnapp hat den Hut verloren!	Schnapp lost his hat!
Sieben hat ihn!	Seven has it!

Immediately number seven answers angrily:

Sieben hat ihn nicht!	Seven doesn't have it!
Fünf hat ihn!	Five has it!

And number five replies:

Fünf hat ihn nicht!	Five doesn't have it!
Drei hat ihn!	Three has it!
etc.	

The game continues, each person calling his own number first and then either a new number or "Schnapp." Players usually try to catch someone unaware and call their number.

When a person misses his turn or doesn't reply correctly, he moves to the right of Schnapp. Each person that was sitting to his left moves up one chair and takes the number of the person who was sitting there before him. The point is to move right, as close to Schnapp as possible, and to get Schnapp out in order to take his place.

• A variation is to have Schnapp let birds fly away instead of having him lose his hat. Hiding places for birds are then used instead of numbers. The person assigned the nest replies:

Die Vögel sind aus dem Nest geflogen; im Erbsenfeld sind sie!	The birds flew out of the nest; they're in the pea patch!

Immediately the person who has been designated as the pea patch says:

Im Erbsenfeld sind sie nicht; auf dem Dache sind sie.	They aren't in the pea patch; they're on the roof.

Then it's the roof's turn, and so on. Other choices of hiding places are the forest (*der Wald*), the garden (*der Garten*), the air (*die Luft*), a telegraph wire (*ein Telegrafendraht*), etc.

15. **Juhe!** (*Juhe* is a Bavarian expression meaning "yea.")

PLAYERS: The whole class.

The class first counts in unison, as far as they wish: *Eins, zwei, drei, vier,* etc. Then the leader explains that the counting will be repeated and when a number can be divided by, say, three, all must add the word *juhe* in unison. Thus: *Eins, zwei, drei, juhe* etc. The game continues, with the group counting as far as they wish in unison.

The game may be played with the individual players counting in rotation, and the appropriate player must add *juhe* if his number is divisible by three. If a player fails to say *juhe,* he is eliminated from the game and the counting goes on until one player is left, who is declared the winner.

The game may be made even more challenging by requiring *juhe* to be added after all multiples of three and all numbers containing a three, or by other versions according to the leader's option.

16. **Der Zahlbaum** (The Number Tree)

PLAYERS: The class or individuals.
NEEDED: A blackboard.

A large tree is drawn on the blackboard and at the end of each branch is a box containing the word for a number.

vier	*fünfzehn*	*zwölf*	*vierzehn*	*zehn*	*eins*
neun	*sechs*	*elf*	*acht*	*drei*	*dreissig*	*sieben*

The object of the game is to see who can add the total of the leaves most quickly and accurately. The class may be divided into teams for a contest for the best mathematician in the class. The teacher changes the numbers on the leaves as the game proceeds to see who can reach the new total first.

• As a variation, the class can find the total of the leaves and then, after erasing the numbers one by one, ascertain the new totals.

17. *Rechnen* (Calculating)

PLAYERS: The class or individuals.

The object of the game is to make as many mathematical combinations of a pre-chosen number as possible within a specified time limit. Each player lists his combinations on a sheet of paper as quickly and accurately as possible. At the end of the time limit, each player must then read aloud in German his list of combinations. Then a new number is chosen.

If the number chosen were ten, the following combinations might be listed:

	Read aloud:
$2 + 8 = 10$	*Zwei und acht ist zehn.*
$20 - 10 = 10$	*Zwanzig minus zehn ist zehn.*
$5 \times 2 = 10$	*Fünf mal zwei ist zehn.*
$11 - 1 = 10$	*Elf minus eins ist zehn.*
$3 + 7 = 10$	*Drei und sieben ist zehn.*
$90 - 80 = 10$	*Neunzig minus achtzig ist zehn.*
etc.	

V

Word Recall and Word Construction Games

18. **Wort-Bingo** (Word Bingo)

AIM: To recognize German equivalents of English words.
PLAYERS: Five to 40.
NEEDED: A list of from 30 to 60 German words with which students are familiar.

Each student draws a box five squares wide and five squares deep. As the words are read off, the student decides which ones he wants to include on his card. He writes each word in a different square until all 25 squares are filled.

Then the teacher selects a word from the list (or draws it from a box) and reads its English equivalent to the class. The student draws an "X" in the box in which the German equivalent is written. When a student has a Bingo, he reads off the five words in German and their English meanings. If all are correct, and all were called by the teacher, he scores a point.

das Haus	das Bein	der Hund	die Sonne	der Elefant
die Maus	die Klasse	die Katze	der Baum	das Heft
der Bleistift	die Kreide	die Schule	der Lehrer	das Papier

das *Auto*	*das* *Gras*	*die* *Farbe*	*das* *Buch*	*der* *Schuh*
die *Bluse*	*das* *Brot*	*der* *Teller*	*das* *Klavier*	*das* *Wort*

19. **Einkaufen** (Shopping)

AIM: To recall and pronounce correctly (with the correct article) items which students might want to buy.
PLAYERS: The whole class.

The first player chooses an item and states in German that he intends to buy it. The next player declares his intention to buy the same item and one other of his own choosing. Each succeeding player must name (in order) all of the items mentioned previously before announcing the one he has chosen to buy.

Ich gehe heute einkaufen und ich kaufe ein Rad.	I am going shopping and I am buying a bicycle.
Ich gehe heute einkaufen und ich kaufe ein Rad und eine Bluse.	I am going shopping and I am buying a bicycle and a blouse.
Ich gehe heute einkaufen und ich kaufe ein Rad und eine Bluse und einen Bleistift.	I am going shopping and I am buying a bicycle and a blouse and a pencil.

Each team member earns a point for every item he can list in the proper order, if it is pronounced correctly and is given with the proper article.

• A variation is to require all persons who make a mistake to sit down, until only one person remains standing, who is declared the winner.

20. **Was ist in der Schachtel?** (What's in the Box?)

AIM: To recall the German names of objects which students have previously seen.
PLAYERS: The whole class.
NEEDED: A group of small objects whose German names are known to the students, a paper bag, and a box.

All players sit in a circle. The leader selects 15 objects and places them in the center of the circle for two minutes. The players try to recall the names of the objects in German. The leader then places all the objects in a paper bag except one, which he places in a box in the center of the circle. He asks someone in the circle what is in the box and the student responds by guessing which one of the 15 objects he believes it to be. If the player is wrong, the leader asks another player what is in the box, and the game continues in the same manner until someone guesses correctly.

Leader:	
Was ist in der Schachtel, Karl?	What's in the box, Karl?
Karl:	
Ist es ein Bleistift?	Is it a pencil?
Leader:	
Nein. Was ist in der Schachtel, Lotte?	No. What's in the box, Lotte?
Lotte:	
Ist es ein Stück Papier?	Is it a piece of paper?
Leader:	
Nein. Was ist in der Schachtel, Thomas?	No. What's in the box, Thomas?

When someone guesses the object, he gets the same number of points as there were incorrect guesses and becomes the new leader. He chooses another object and the game continues.

• As a variation, the leader can give a clue to the object after each incorrect guess.

21. *Losungswort mit Mannschaften*   (Password with Teams)

AIM: To determine a German word from one-word clues in German.

PLAYERS: The class is divided into two teams.

Each team chooses a leader, and both leaders are shown the same German word, which their teammates must guess. First one leader gives his team a one-word clue in German and his team may venture one guess about the word in question. Then the other leader gives a one-word clue in German to his team, which also has one chance to guess the word. The game continues, alternating between the teams, until one of the teams guesses the word, thereby winning a point.

• As a variation, the team members can give the clues and the leaders do the guessing.

22. *Losungswort mit Partnern* (Password with Partners)

AIM: To determine German words from one-word clues in German.

PLAYERS: The whole class, each student with a partner.

The students form two parallel rows so that each student stands in line across from his partner. The students in Row One decide secretly on a word which their partners in the opposite row will have to guess. The contest starts at the end of Row One as a student gives his partner in Row Two a one-word clue in German to the word decided upon. His partner responds with the German word he believes Row One has chosen.

If he is correct, he and his partner win a point. If not, the second person in Row One gives a one-word clue to *his* partner. His partner then ventures one guess as to what the word in question is. The game continues in this manner until someone guesses the word, based on all of the preceding clues, thereby winning a point for him and his partner.

Once the word has been guessed by a partner in Row Two, Row Two decides on the next German word to be guessed and Row One does the guessing.

23. *Leerer Raum* (Blank Space)

AIM: To recall words missing from sentences in previous German conversations.

PLAYERS: The class is divided into two teams.

Each team chooses two members as "contestants" and one as a "monitor." The contestants stand in front of their own team and the monitor of the opposing team stands between them. A member from Team One gives contestants from Team Two a sentence from a previous German conversation. He substitutes the word "blank" for the German word which he chooses to omit from the sentence, as follows:

Meine Lieblingsfarbe ist blank.   My favorite color is ————.
Wie blank *es Dir heute?*   How are you today? (The
                                     missing word is *geht*.)

Each of the Team Two contestants writes down on a separate piece of paper the word he thinks is missing in the sentence. If both contestants write down exactly the same word, the monitor writes it on the board as they have spelled it. If the word is correct, and is also spelled correctly, Team Two receives a point. Then a member of Team Two gives a sentence to the contestants of Team One, etc.

• As a variation, the team member directs a statement (to the contestants of the opposing team) which can be completed with one word.

24. *Wortbilde* (Word Picture)

AIM: To understand the component parts of German words through pictograms (*Wortbilder*).
PLAYERS: The Class is divided into two teams.
NEEDED: Blackboard and chalk.

Each team makes up several *Wortbilder* or picture representations of words or phrases, as in the following:

$$+ \qquad O \qquad = \qquad Schneeball$$
$$Schnee \qquad Ball$$

If a drawing is ambiguous, the English words might be written in parentheses alongside the pictures.

To start the game, a member of Team One goes to the board and draws one of his team's *Wortbilder*. After the *Wortbild* is completed, Team Two has one minute to determine what German word the *Wortbild* stands for. If the team guesses correctly, it scores a point. The game proceeds as Team Two draws a *Wortbild* and Team One attempts to guess the German word it represents.

25. *Zeichne!* (Draw!)

AIM: To associate German words with illustrations.
PLAYERS: The class is divided into two teams.
NEEDED: A blackboard and chalk.

A member of Team One calls on a member of Team Two in German to draw an object:
Zeichne eine Kuh. Draw a cow.

The object should be one whose German equivalent is familar to the class, and the student has 30 seconds to sketch it on the board. If his picture representation indicates that he knows the meaning of the German word, he scores a point for his team. The game continues, alternating between teams.

26. *Buchstabenaustausch* (Letter Exchange)

AIM: To construct German words from scrambled letters.
PLAYERS: The class is divided into two teams.
NEEDED: Ten small squares of paper for each student.

The two teams face each other. Each person thinks of a German word no more than ten letters long and writes each letter that makes up the word on one of the little pieces of paper. When everyone has done this, team members exchange their letters with the person across from them on the opposing team. Each student immediately tries to figure out his opponent's word by arranging the letters in the proper order. Each person who unscrambles the letters of his counterpart on the opposing team before the latter can unscramble his wins a point for his team.

27. *Anagramme* (Anagrams)

AIM: To construct German words from scrambled letters.
PLAYERS: Five to forty.
NEEDED: A mimeographed list of ten to 20 scrambled words, such as the following:

Muba	(*Baum*)	Tree
Trilech	(*Lichter*)	Lights
Fenplaz	(*Pflanze*)	Plant

The teacher hands out a mimeographed list to each student. The first student to correctly unscramble all the words on the list wins.

28. *Kreuzwörter*   (Crosswords)

AIM: To construct words in German.
PLAYERS: Teams of no more than four students.
NEEDED: A piece of graph paper for each team.

Each team has a piece of graph paper on which the same word is written, one letter to a square, in the center of the sheet. Each team attempts to construct a crossword puzzle—without numbers and the like—by building from or onto the word in the middle. At the end of 30 minutes, each team counts the number of words contained in its puzzle and receives a point for each different word. Five points are lost for each misspelled word.

29. *Wortjagd*   (Word Hunt)

AIM: To recall German words for things in the classroom, given the first letter of each word.
PLAYERS: The class is divided into two teams.
NEEDED: A blackboard and chalk.

The teacher puts two identical lists of letters in a vertical column on the blackboard, and both teams compete simultaneously. The first student of each team advances to the blackboard and writes the name of something in the room which begins with the first letter. The second person in the team goes to the board and writes the name of something in the room which begins with the second letter, and so on. The first team to use all the letters wins five points. Each team is also awarded two points for each word spelled correctly.

Students are permitted to help their classmates when their whole team is seated; however, they may not assist a teammate once he has advanced to the board.

30. *Alphabetschiff* (Alphabet Ship)

AIM: To recall an object in German, beginning with a given letter. (The game lends itself particularly well to practicing plural forms of nouns.)

PLAYERS: Ten or more.

One player starts by telling what he sells in his store, and this item must begin with "a," the first letter of the alphabet. A player from the opposing team then says he is selling an item which begins with the letter "b," and so on through the alphabet. (Letters "q," "x," and "y" may be omitted.)

1st Player, Team One:

In meinem Laden verkaufe   In my store I sell apples.
    ich Äpfel.

1st Player, Team Two:

In meinem Laden verkaufe   In my store I sell books.
    ich Bücher.

Each player who can contribute scores a point.

• As a variation, choose only one letter of the alphabet.

31. *Die Pyramide* (The Pyramid)

AIM: To recall as many German words as possible which begin with a given letter.

PLAYERS: Any number.

A word with from five to ten letters is chosen—say, for example, the word *fahren*. Each student writes the word vertically on a piece of paper. Then, starting with the second letter of the vertical work, he writes a two-letter German word beginning with the letter "a." He continues downward, making each succeeding word longer by one letter than the last one.

F
AN
HEU
RAUM
ERNTE
NICHTS

• As a variation, the student writes the same letter repeatedly in a vertical column on a piece of paper. He then fills the sheet with words which *end* in that letter, each of which grows longer by one letter downward toward the base.

S

ES

DAS

HASS

BLASS

32. *Darf ich vorstellen?*   (May I Introduce?)

AIM: To recall as many German words as possible which begin with a given letter.

PLAYERS: Up to 20.

NEEDED: A blackboard and chalk.

A player goes to the blackboard and says:

Darf ich Ihnen meinen	May I introduce you to
Freund Karl vorstellen?	my friend, Karl?

He then writes on the board the letters of the name of his friend, in this manner:

K   A   R   L

In a given time, students must write as many words as they can that begin with each letter of the name:

Käse	*an*	*Raum*	*los*
Kamera	*aus*	*Reim*	*lustig*
Küche	*Angst*	*rot*	*laut*
		rauben	*Lärm*
		richtig	

The teacher may set the rules for what kind of words are acceptable: only one form of a given verb, no proper names, etc. The player who has the longest list of words within a given time limit is declared the winner. If there is more time, another introduction and corresponding wordlists may be made in the same way.

33. **A, B, C**

> AIM: To think of as many German words as possible which begin with the same letter.
>
> PLAYERS: From two to eight teams of five members each.

Each team is given a letter of the alphabet and has 15 minutes to think of as many words as possible that begin with that letter. The team with the longest list of correctly spelled German words at the end of the 15 minutes wins.

34. **Golf**

> AIM: To recall the shortest German word possible when two letters are given.
>
> PLAYERS: From one to 40, each student playing individually.
>
> NEEDED: A German text or reader.

Each student has a piece of paper on which he writes the numbers 1 through 9 vertically on the left side. He then opens the book to a page selected at random. He copies the first two letters of the first line of the German text opposite number 1 on his paper, etc., through the ninth line. When each of the nine *Löcher* (holes) of the golf course has two letters beside it, he is ready to play the course.

To the two letters for *Loch* 1 (such as "r" and "o"), he adds others before, after, or in between to make the shortest word possible. When he has written a word for *Loch* 1, he goes on to *Loch* 2, and so on around the course, trying to complete the nine holes in as few "strokes" as possible; that is, to have the lowest total possible for the words that represent each hole.

• As a variation, an eighteen-hole match can be played, proceeding in the same manner, by using the first two letters of the first 18 lines of the book.

35. **Viele Wörter aus einem** (Many Words from One)

> AIM: To construct as many words as possible from a given group of letters.
>
> PLAYERS: Any number.

The teacher presents the class with a word or phrase or sentence. Students rearrange the letters to form new German words. The player with the longest list of correct words is the winner.

The following is an example of words derived from rearranging the letters in the word *Bein: ein, in, nie, bin.*

36. *Buchstabenhaufen*   (Letter Pile)

AIM: To construct German words, given certain letters.
PLAYERS: The class is divided into two teams.
NEEDED: A pile of little pieces of paper with a letter from the German alphabet on each piece.

To start, each member of one team draws two pieces of paper, sits down, and places the two pieces—letter-side up—on top of his desk. While this team remains seated, each member of the opposing team draws two letters from the letter pile and then goes over to look at the letters on the desks of the other team. Each player on the team that is standing tries to use the letters of an opponent, in combination with his own, to form a German word. If he can make a word by using both of an opposing member's letters and at least one of his own, he takes this person's letters back to his desk with him.

When time is called, each member of the team that is standing chooses two more letters from the letter pile, sits down, and puts his word (if he has been able to construct one) and his two new letters face up on his desk. (He is not allowed to make any changes by using his two new letters.)

The seated team now has its chance to obtain letters. Players on this team stand, draw two new letters each, and attempt to make words in combination with the unused letters of an opponent. Letters may be won from an opponent only if the person who is standing can make a word by using at least one of his own letters. If the opponent has made a word, this can be won only by adding on a letter to make a new word or new form of the word. If the letters on the desk are not being used to make a word and a person who is standing can make a word by using the letters in combination with his own, he can take the letters he needs.

At the end, each team receives a point for each letter which contributes to a word. Letters that don't belong to a word or that belong to a word which is incorrect do not count. The winning team is the team with the most points.

37. *Wort ohne Kopf*   (Word without a Head)

AIM: To think of German words which, without their first
           letter, constitute another German word.
PLAYERS: Any number.

Each player writes a word and forms another word by "decapitating" the first one, as in the following examples:

fuhr – Uhr;   Preis – Reis;   Herde – Erde

He thinks of as many such words as he can within 15 minutes.

A player scores one point for each correct word and forfeits two points for any nonexistent word appearing in his list.

38. *Auf die Leiter*   (Up the Ladder)

AIM: To recall German words which contain a given letter
           combination or pertain to a given topic.
PLAYERS: The class is divided into teams of from seven to ten
           players each.
NEEDED: A blackboard and chalk.

Each player has a turn writing a word and "climbing" his team's ladder as quickly as possible. But all of the players first agree on the kind of words to be written; for example, words containing a certain letter of the alphabet, or colors, etc. Each team captain draws a "ladder" on the blackboard with ten "steps" numbered consecutively from the bottom.

The game begins as the first player in each team runs to the board and fills the bottom space of his team's ladder with a word that fits the chosen category. When the first player on a team has returned to his seat, the second player rushes to the board to put in the second word on the ladder, and so on. When one team has filled its ladder with ten words, it receives a point for finishing first, and the game stops.

Each team is awarded a point for every correct word in its list, and the team with the most points is the winner.

As a follow up, students may take turns using the words in the ladder in sentences. Then another category of words may be chosen for another round. Models of the top halves of ladders whose words must contain the diphthong "au" might look like this:

10. *Auto*	10.
9. *ausser*	9.
8. *aus*	8. *automatisch*
7. *Haus*	7. *Mauer*
6. *braun*	6. *laut*
5. *Bau*	5. *aus*
(1 + 6 = 7 points)	(4 points)

39. *Das gleiche Wort*   (The Same Word)

AIM: To answer questions in one word.
PLAYERS: The class is divided into two teams.

Each team captain sits in front of his team and the teams take turns asking questions of the captains that can be answered in one word. For example, a member of Team One might ask:

Welche Farbe ist ihr Lieblingshemd?   (What color is your favorite shirt?)

Each captain writes down his answer on a scrap of paper and all players write down the answer they think their captain will write. Each captain then reads his answer. A team scores a point for each team member who answers with the same word as his captain.

Then a member of Team Two asks a question of the captains, and the game continues in this manner for 15 minutes or until a team has scored 40 points.

40. *Deine Note ist meine.*   (Your Grade is Mine.)

AIM: To give the English equivalent for German words from previous lessons.
PLAYERS: The class is divided into pairs.

Everyone writes ten different words from a recent assignment and exchanges the list with someone else. Each person gets two minutes to look up the meanings for the words he doesn't know on the list. Then the students pair off with someone who hasn't seen their lists and have five minutes to define the ten words to their partners. A player says the word in German (if the teacher desires), then defines the word in German, and the partner writes the English equivalent of the word. At the end of five minutes the students' papers are graded. The person who read the words in German gets whatever grade his partner receives on the test.

41. *Auf Deutsch*   (In German)

AIM: To recall the German equivalents of English words.
PLAYERS: The whole class.

The whole class stands and the teacher gives a student a word in English, to which he must respond with the correct German word. If he misses, he must sit down. Students are asked similar words in order of the seating arrangement. The last five students left standing score a point. (This is a good way to conduct or correct a long vocabulary test.)

42. *Wer kann schwimmen?*   (Who Can Swim?)

AIM: To recall the meanings of German nouns from previous lessons and to practice placement of the word *nicht* in sentences.
PLAYERS: The class is divided into two teams.
NEEDED: A blackboard.

The game is played as a spelldown between two teams. The leader reads from, or writes on, the blackboard a list of words that include live and inanimate objects—beginning, for example, with *die Katze*. The first player on the first team must answer:
Die Katze kann schwimmen.   The cat can swim.
   If the word were an *inanimate* object, like *die Tinte*, he would answer:

Die Tinte kann nicht schwimmen.   The ink can't swim.

If a player fails to answer within a given time, or answers incorrectly, he is out of the game. Then a player on the other team tries to answer correctly, using the next word in the list. The leader should start with familiar words and go on to those that are less well known. The team with the most players at the end of the game is the winner.

VI

Object Identification Games

43. *Packesel* (Baggage Mule)

AIM: To identify objects in German.
PLAYERS: The whole class.
NEEDED: Common objects which are unbreakable.

One person (*der Packesel*) is blindfolded and wanders about within a circle formed by his classmates, each of whom holds an unbreakable object whose German name is familiar to the class. The *Packesel* stops in front of someone and says:

Was soll ich tragen?   What should I carry?

The person then puts an article in his hand, but the *Packesel* is permitted to hold and feel the object with only one hand as he tries to identify it in German. If he does not guess it in three tries, he must carry it around the circle until his time (set by teacher) is up.

44. *Sammlung in einem Sack*   (Collection in a Sack)

AIM: To collect and identify familar objects in German.
PLAYERS: The class is divided into two teams or pairs.
NEEDED: A sack for each team.

The players look for objects, within a given time, which they place into the sack. Out-of-doors objects might be seeds, twigs, flowers, stones, etc. Indoor objects might be buttons, a piece of chalk, a book, a pencil, etc. At the end of the time limit, each group or pair tries to name each item in the sack in German, scoring one point for each object correctly identified. The game may also be played with a cup, or even a thimble, instead of a sack.

45. *Die Schüssel*   (The Bowl)

AIM: To identify small objects in German and to practice the accusative case by using direct objects.

PLAYERS: The whole class.

NEEDED: Several small articles for each student, such as a coin or key, and a record player, a record of German songs, and a plastic bowl.

A German song is played while an empty plastic bowl is passed around by the players who are sitting in a circle. When the music stops, the person who holds the bowl at that moment must show the others what he will put in the bowl as a forfeit, and he must name it in German. For example:

Ich lege einen Bleistift   I am placing a pencil
   in die Schüssel.   in the bowl.

The music is resumed and the bowl is again passed around the circle. When the music stops, the player who is holding the bowl must likewise pay a forfeit.

At the end of the song, the player who has the bowl holds up the forfeits for the group to see, and says:

Ich behalte alle Sachen die ich   I am keeping all of the things
   nennen kann.   that I can name.

He keeps as many objects as he can correctly name in German. The group corrects him in chorus, and the unnamed forfeits, plus those incorrectly identified, remain in the bowl and are passed around the circle as before.

46. *Im Beutel*   (In the Bag)

AIM: To identify items contained in a sack in German.
PLAYERS: The class is divided into two or more teams.
NEEDED: A bag and a group of objects furnished by each team.

Each team prepares a bag with a predetermined number of objects which classmates should be able to identify correctly in German. The teams exchange bags, and the team which first identifies everything in the bag correctly wins.

47. *Das Tuch ist ab!*   (The Cloth Is Off!)

AIM: To correctly identify objects in German.
PLAYERS: The class is divided into teams or by individuals.
NEEDED: Objects the students should be able to identify correctly in German, and a sheet or large cloth.

The objects are placed under the cloth by the teacher so that no one can see what they are. When the cloth is removed, the teacher says:

Das Tuch ist ab!   The cloth is off!
Was lag darunter?   What was lying underneath?

The team that can correctly identify the greatest number of objects in German wins. The game is usually timed.

48. *Unter dem Tuch*   (Under the Cloth)

AIM: To identify in German objects which students have just seen.
PLAYERS: Any number.
NEEDED: A table, cloth, and a number of objects, such as a coin, pin, book, pen, etc.

When the players enter the room, a number of small objects will be seen on the table, but the leader will make no mention of them. In the middle of the session, the leader will cover the table with a cloth and say:

Was liegt unter dem Tuch?   What is lying under the cloth?

The players must then write the names of as many objects as they can recall in German. The one with the longest list of German words correctly written is the winner.

For those with less knowledge of German, the objects on the table may be inspected and identified by tags with the names printed in German. Possible objects are: *die Münze* (coin), *der Bleistift* (pencil), *das Buch* (book), *der Füller* (fountain pen), *das Heft* (notebook), etc.

49. *Ich sehe was*   (I See Something)

AIM: To name everything of a given color within sight in the classroom.

PLAYERS: The whole class.

A player who is selected to be the leader says:

Ich sehe was, was du nicht siehst.	I see something that you don't see.

He then names the color of the object and the other players try to guess the object by naming everything in the classroom which is that color, as in the following example.

Leader:
Es ist rot.	It is red.

Player 1:
Ist es Karls Bleistift?	Is it Karl's pencil?

Player 2:
Ist es das Wörterbuch?	Is it the dictionary?

Player 3:
Ist es das Lineal?	Is it the ruler?
etc.	

The player who identifies the object correctly in German takes the leader's place. He decides on a new object, gives its color, and the guessing continues in German.

50. *Was fiel?* (What Fell?)

AIM: To identify objects in German.

PLAYERS: The whole class.

NEEDED: About ten objects that can be dropped without breaking and a carton for them (suggested objects: *Messer* (knife), *Gabel* (fork). *Schuh* (shoe), etc.)

The players turn their backs and listen as the leader takes each article from the carton and drops it to the floor. To introduce the players to the game, the leader may drop a knife and say:

> *Fiel ein Messer, eine Gabel*   Did a knife, fork,
> *oder ein Schuh?*   or shoe fall?

The players write on their papers the name of the object they believe was dropped. Then the leader proceeds with another object, each time naming several choices for what was dropped.

At the end of the game, the players turn around and face the leader with their lists. The leader repeats the dropping of the articles, which can now be seen, naming aloud each object so that the players may check their lists. The player with the most correct answers wins. The game may also be played with oral answers instead of written ones.

51. *Schaffner* (Conductor)

AIM: To identify pictures of objects in German.

PLAYERS: The whole class.

NEEDED: Flashcards, each with picture of a person or an object already familiar to students in German, such as *der Junge, der Baum*, etc.

The players sit in chairs arranged in rows. One player is chosen as *der Schaffner* and stands behind one of the player's chairs. The leader shows a card with a picture and the player in the chair tries to say the German word for the object before the *Schaffner*, standing behind him, can do so. A score is kept.

In the next round, the *Schaffner* stands behind the chair of the next student and the game continues.

• As a variation, the *Schaffner* receives a point each time he is able to respond correctly before the person in the chair, and when another player beats the *Schaffner*, he becomes the new *Schaffner*.

52. *Im Kreis*   (In the Circle)

AIM:　　To identify in German objects which students have just seen.

PLAYERS:　The class is divided into two teams.

NEEDED:　A cord or rope and a number of small objects whose names are familiar to the players.

A circle is formed with the rope, and while the players turn their backs the leader places several (five or six) of the objects within the circle. Both teams are then permitted 15 seconds to observe the objects. They again turn their backs on the circle and each team lists in German the names of the objects seen, as many as its members can recall. One point is scored for each article correctly listed. The game can be repeated for several rounds as different collections of objects are used each time. The team with the most points is the winner.

53. *Was fehlt?*   (What's Missing?)

AIM:　　To identify in German items which are missing in a picture.

PLAYERS:　The class is divided into teams.

NEEDED:　A mimeographed drawing with certain things left out, such as a person's eye, the roof of a house, etc.

After each student receives one of the mimeographed sheets, the teams have five minutes to list in German as many of the missing items as they can. At the end of the time limit, the team with the longest list of missing items wins.

54. *Welches Bild fehlt?*   (Which Picture Is Missing?)

AIM: To identify in German real or pictured objects.
PLAYERS: The class is divided into two or more teams.
NEEDED: Five real or pictured objects.

The objects are set in front of the class. Then the students cover their eyes while the leader takes one of the objects away. The teacher then indicates that the students may look, and the first team to tell in German which object is missing gets a point.

55. *Das ist*   (That Is)

AIM: To identify real or pictured objects correctly in German.
PLAYERS: The class is divided into two teams.
NEEDED: A box of objects or a stack of flashcards with drawings of familiar objects.

In spelling-bee fashion, the teams try to correctly identify, in German, real or pictured objects which the teacher holds up. When someone misses, he must sit down. The team which remains standing longer wins.

56. *Zeig mal!*   (Show Me!)

AIM: To name objects in German which a student sees in the classroom.
PLAYERS: The whole class.

A student stands in front of the class and asks the students where something is, for example:
Wo ist die Tafel?   Where is the blackboard?
His classmates respond by pointing to the object named. The student gets a point for each different German object which he correctly asks his classmates to locate. When he makes a mistake in pronunciation or in using the article, he must call on someone else to take his place in front of the class. The student with the most points at the end of a given time period wins.

57. *Das Bild*   (The Picture)

AIM: To identify in German as many items as possible in a
           given picture.

PLAYERS: The class is divided into teams, or by individuals.

NEEDED: One large picture, or several pictures, easily visible to
           the entire class.

Each team names or lists on paper, and in German, as many items
in the picture or pictures as it can correctly identify. The teams score
one point for each item correctly identified.

58. *Aufschriften*   (Labels)

AIM: To apply the correct German labels to drawings of
           objects.

PLAYERS: The class is divided into teams, or by individuals.

NEEDED: A mimeographed list of German labels for familiar
           objects and a mimeographed sheet with pictures of
           the objects contained in the list.

The teacher passes out the mimeographed list of objects to each
student and gives them several minutes to study it. Then the students
are asked to put the lists away (unless the teacher prefers to let
students use the list) and each team receives a mimeographed sheet
of paper on which are drawn the items contained in the list. The
drawings are not in the same order as the words in the list, however,
and the teams compete to see which one can correctly label all of the
drawings in German first. If individuals are competing, the first
player who finishes the labeling correctly wins.

VII

Category Games

59. *Deutsche Namen* (German Names)

AIM: To practice German first names.
PLAYERS: The class is divided into two teams, the boys on one
          and the girls on the other.
NEEDED: A blackboard.

The headings *Jungen* and *Mädchen* are written on the board. As
students raise their hands and call out a German name, the leader
at the blackboard writes the names under the appropriate headings.
The team which has the greater number of German names at the
end of a set time limit is the winner.

60. *Der Körper* (The Body)

AIM: To practice naming parts of the body in German.
PLAYERS: The class is divided into two teams.

The two lines of players face each other and a player from one team
says:
    Dies ist mein Finger—   This is my finger—
        eins, zwei, drei, vier . . .   one, two three, four . . .
Before he reaches ten, a player on the opposite side must point to
another part of the body, such as his ear, and say:
    Dies ist mein Ohr—   This is my ear—
        eins, zwei, drei, vier . . .   one, two, three, four . . .

35

Then the next player on the first team must begin to speak before the count of ten.

The game continues in this manner through both teams. A player who fails to answer in time must drop out. The winning team is the one with more players remaining at the end of the game.

61. *Kofferpacken*   (Packing the Suitcase)

> AIM: To practice naming clothes in German.
> PLAYERS: The class is divided into two teams.
> NEEDED: A suitcase or large box or carton.

The first person on a team lays shoes in the suitcase and says *Schuhe*. The first member on the opposing team repeats the word *Schuhe* and puts something else, a handkerchief perhaps, in the suitcase, saying *Taschentuch*. The next person on the starting team says *Schuhe, Taschentuch,* and puts a third item in the suitcase, also saying the name of this object in German. This continues in alternation between the teams.

When a person cannot find an object which he can identify in German, or cannot identify the objects in the suitcase correctly, his team forfeits its turn. When a person can identify all the objects correctly and add an item, his team wins a point. The team with the most points at the end of the game wins.

62. *Kategorienliste*   (List of Categories)

> AIM: To name German words in a prescribed category.
> PLAYERS: The class is divided into two teams.

Start with a category such as animals, objects in a living room, etc. Alternating back and forth between teams, team members take turns naming a German word in the prescribed category. When a player on one team can't think of another word, the last team to contribute gets a point. The game then continues, with the same category or a new one.

• As a variation, teams can work simultaneously at making a list of words which fit the category.

After one minute, the team with the longer list gets a point.

63. *Es lebt* (It Lives)

AIM: To list in German the names of living things.
PLAYERS: An individual or a group.
NEEDED: A blackboard or large paper on which is printed the word *lebt* in this manner:

L   E   B   T

The object of the game is to see how many lving things or persons may be written under each letter of the word *lebt*. Students may use a dictionary, and proper names may be written. After a given time, the person with the longest list is the winner.

The list on the blackboard might look as follows:

L	E	B	T
Löwe	*Esel*	*Bohne*	*Truthahn*
Leonhard	*Elefant*	*Bär*	*Tomate*
	Elsa	*Beere*	*Thomas*
	Erbsen		*Theodore*

64. *Es fliegt!* (It Flies!)

AIM: To practice German words for things that fly.
PLAYERS: The whole class.

Students stand at their desks. The leader stands in front and calls:
   Alle Vögel fliegen hoch.   All the birds are flying high.
The players all put up their arms.

Now the leader calls out different animals or things, the majority of which fly, such as the following:

der Vögel	*der Hubschrauber*
die Fliege	*die Biene*
das Flugzeug	*die Hummel*
das Raumschiff	*der Schmetterling*
die Rakete	*die Motte*
der Drachen	*der Maikäfer*
der Star	*der Adler*
die Wanze	*die Gans*
die Mücke	*die Ente*
die Eule	*der Rabe*
der Marienkäfer	*die Taube*

The students' arms fly up if the object named can fly. But when the leader names something that does not fly, no one should lift his arms except the leader. If someone does this mistakenly, he must sit down. The last five students to remain standing win.

65. *Die Treppe*   (The Staircase)

AIM: To list words of a given category in German.
PLAYERS: The class is divided into two teams or participates as individuals.

Each student draws a staircase with at least four steps on a piece of paper. The teacher names a category, such as parts of the body, furniture, colors, etc., and tells each student to draw an object that belongs to the given category on the top step, labeling it correctly in German. The students then have one minute to fill each of the steps with a German word pertaining to the given category. After one minute has passed, students or teams receive one point for each step in the staircase correctly filled.

For example, if the category *Tiere* were chosen, the stairs might look as follows:

                                            das Pferd
                        das Schwein
            der Hund
    die Katze

As a variation, the stairs can be labeled with words that have the same initial letter, with words that have certain letter combinations, such as *au* or *st*. or with words that belong to the same word family, as follows:

                                            der Baum
                        der Tannenbaum
            der Baumstamm
    der Baumgarten

The main word of each word family should be the word on the top stair.

66. *Die Früchte* (Fruits)

AIM: To practice naming fruits in German.
PLAYERS: The whole class.

The leader whispers the name of a fruit to each player and remembers one for himself. No one is supposed to know the name of each other's fruit. Then two players act as *der Engel* and *der Teufel*. The angel approaches a player and says:

Angel:	*Klopf, klopf.*	Knock, knock.
Player:	*Wer ist's?*	Who's there?
Angel:	*Der Engel mit dem goldenen Becher.*	The angel with the golden chalice.
Player:	*Was willst du?*	What do you want?
Angel:	*Ich will Früchte.*	I want fruit.
Player:	*Was für Früchte?*	What kind of fruit?

The angel then guesses the name of a fruit. If he guesses correctly, the player becomes a member of his team and steps to one side. If the angel does not guess correctly, he waits until the devil has had a turn. The *Engel* and *Teufel* alternate until all the players are on one team or the other.

When the *Teufel* knocks, he says in answer to "Who's there?"

| *Der Teufel mit den vierzigtausend Hörnern.* | The devil with 40,000 horns. |

67. *Ausschließung* (Elimination)

AIM: To name German words of a given topic.
PLAYERS: The class is divided into two teams.
NEEDED: A blackboard.

The whole class stands up and the teacher states a topic—such as plants, things in a classroom, or parts of the body—for which the students know many words in German. In order of the seating arrangement, each student offers a word that fits the topic. The teacher keeps a cumulative list of these words on the blackboard. When a student cannot think of a new word, or makes a mistake in the word he offers, or hesitates too long, he must sit down. The last five students who remain standing score a point.

If the topic doesn't have many words, the teacher can determine ahead of time how many words he wants in the list, and when that number is reached all students who are still standing score a point. The teacher begins a new topic with the whole class standing.

68. *Der Stein*   (The Stone)

AIM: To name German words of a given topic.
PLAYERS: The whole class.
NEEDED: A stone or other small object.

The players, 15 or more, sit in a circle. The leader puts a stone in a player's hand and then says:

Nenne sechs Vögel.   Name six birds.

This player must start passing the stone around the circle and begin calling off the names of birds. He must name six different birds before the stone goes completely around the circle to score a point. Then the leader puts the stone in another player's hand, names a new topic, and the same process continues.

69. *Kategorien unter einem Wort*   (Categories under a Word)

AIM: To list German words which apply to specified categories.
PLAYERS: Any number.
NEEDED: A square-filled blackboard or mimeographed sheets.

A German word is written across the top and a category is listed for each horizontal row of squares. The number of vertical columns will depend on the number of letters in the word at the top.

Each player must fill in as many words as possible in each space within an allotted time. Each word must begin with the letter at the top and belong to the category listed on the left. The player with the most words is the winner.

A completed sheet might look like this:

	H	U	N	D
Knabenname	*Hubert*	*Ulbricht*	*Norbert*	*Daniel*
Mädchenname	*Henriette*	*Ursula*	*Nellie*	*Dora*
Natur	*Himbeere*	*Ulme*	*Nelke*	*Dorn*
Klasse	*Heft*	*Uhr*	*Nachbar*	*Decke*
Städte	*Hamburg*	*Unterammergau*	*Nürnberg*	*Düsseldorf*

VIII

Asking and Answering Games

70. *Ich wähle* (I Choose)

AIM: To review vocabulary by using German words in sentences.

PLAYERS: The whole class.

NEEDED: A picture containing a number of identifiable objects.

Each player looks at the picture and announces three choices, as in the following example:

> *Ich wähle das Rad, die Katze*   I choose the bicycle, the cat,
> *und die Tasche.*   and the purse.

He then writes each of his choices in a German sentence.

The pictures may be of random objects or of articles within a given category, such as food, clothing, or the like.

71. *Satz ohne Subjekt* (Sentence without a Subject)

AIM: To supply a subject for a German sentence, given the predicate.

PLAYERS: The class is divided into two teams.

NEEDED: Cards or slips of paper on which is written only the predicate of a sentence (one slip for each player).

The slips of paper are placed in a container. Alternating between teams each player must go to the container and draw a slip, read the half-sentence that is written on it, and add a subject and repeat the sentence correctly. For example:

. . . *sind Geschwister.*	. . . are brother and sister.
Karl und Jutta sind Geschwister.	Karl and Judy are brother and sister.

If the subject is reasonable and fits grammatically in the sentence, the player scores a point for his team. The game continues until each player has drawn a slip and completed a sentence. The team with the most points at the end of the game wins.

72. *Bilderfragen* (Picture Questions)

AIM: To answer questions asked about a picture.
PLAYERS: The class is divided into two teams.
NEEDED: A picture large enough for the whole class to see distinctly.

The leader asks questions of individual students, alternating from one team to the other. For example:

Wie viele Jungen siehst du auf dem Bild?	How many boys do you see in the picture?
Welche Farbe ist das Auto, links?	What color is the car on the left?

Each correct answer scores a point for the team. If a player fails to answer correctly, the other team gets a chance at the question.

• As a variation, simple pictures of several animals can be used with such questions as:

Wie viele grosse Tiere siehst du?	How many large animals do you see?
Welches Tier ist das kleinste?	Which animal is the smallest?

73. *Das Geschenk* (The Present)

AIM: To practice sentences that explain purpose or intention.
PLAYERS: The whole class.

Each student whispers to his neighbor on the right what present he will give him. For example:

Ich gebe dir eine Mundharmonika.	I'm giving you a harmonica.
Ich gebe dir eine Zahnbürste.	I'm giving you a toothbrush.

Then he turns to his neighbor on the left and whispers what he can do with the present. For example:

Ich gebe dir etwas zum Spielen.	I'm giving you something to play with.
Ich gebe dir etwas zum Bürsten.	I'm giving you something to brush with.

Then each person tells what he has been given, and what he must do with it in a complete German sentence. He calls on someone to translate his sentence by saying:

Karl, bitte, auf englisch, was habe ich bekommen und was soll ich damit tun?	Karl, please tell me in English what I have received and what I should do with it?

Since there is rarely a logical relationship between the presents and their use, the combined statements are often quite humorous.

74. *Reimspiel* (Rhyming Game)

AIM: To compose a simple four-line poem, given the rhyming words at the end of each line.

PLAYERS: Any number.

Each person writes four words—two pairs that rhyme—in a column on the right-hand side of a piece of paper; for example, the words *Filz, Pilz,* and *Hans, Tanz.* His neighbor is given the piece of paper and must make up four lines that use the specified words to end each line. For example:

Da ist eine Maus.	There is a mouse.
Sie wohnt in dem Haus.	He lives in the house.
Ihre Augen sind rot.	His eyes are red.
Sie isst unser Brot.	He eats our bread.

75. *Warum - weil*   (Why - Because)

AIM: To construct German sentences using the conjunction *weil*.

PLAYERS: The class is divided into two teams.

Everyone must write a question that begins with *warum* on a piece of paper. For example:

Warum bist du heute so spät gekommen?	Why did you come so late today?
Warum schläfst du gern?	Why do you like to sleep?

When everyone is finished, he folds his piece of paper and passes it to his neighbor on the right.

Now everyone writes a statement beginning with *weil*, such as:

weil der Bus so spät kam.	because the bus was so late.
weil ich immer müde bin.	because I'm always tired.

Then everyone lays his piece of paper in a common pile and draws a new one, which he must read as a completed sentence. He also translates the sentence into English. If the German sentence and the translation are correct, he wins two points for his team. Again, the combinations usually turn out to be quite humorous.

76. *Was - wenn*   (What - When)

AIM: To construct sentences beginning with *Was würdest du tun, wenn...*

PLAYERS: The class is divided into two teams.

The game is played as above, but sentences will follow these sample patterns:

Question:

Was würdest du tun, wenn du hungrig wärest?	What would you do if you were hungry?

Answer:

Ich würde essen, wenn ich hungrig wäre.	I would eat if I were hungry.

77. *Schneller Satz* (Quick Sentence)

AIM: To compose a German sentence, given the first letter of each word.

PLAYERS: The whole class.

The class decides how many and which letters to choose, but they need not all be different. If, for example, "w," "b," "d," "h," "s," and "b" were chosen, these letters would be used—in order—as the first letter for each word. Everyone has ten minutes to compose a sentence which has meaning. Sentences that use the six letters of our example might read:

Warum bist du heute so böse?   Why are you so angry today?
Warum beißt der Hase sein   Why is the rabbit biting his
   Bein?   leg?

The first player to complete a sentence hands it to the teacher. When the teacher has eight sentences, she calls the game to an end (two of the eight sentences might be from one student). She reads the sentences, or writes them on the board, and the students decide if there are any errors in them. For each correct sentence, the student who wrote it receives a point. Then new letters are chosen and the game continues.

The same thing can be done by composing an ad or a telegram, or making other restrictions as to the type of sentence.

78. *Wer? Wo? Wann? Was?* (Who? Where? When? What?)

AIM: To compose answers to questions asked by a leader.

PLAYERS: The whole class.

The leader asks a question that begins with *wer* and can be answered with the name of a person. Everyone then writes the answer at the top of a piece of paper, using the name of a person who is known to everyone in the class. The question might be:

Wer ist der best Sportler   Who is the best athlete
   in der Schule?   in the school?

Each person then folds his paper so that the name is concealed and passes the paper to his neighbor. The leader then asks a question beginning with *wo*, such as:

Wo wohnt er?   Where does he live?

Everyone writes down the answer, folds down the paper over it, and again passes it on.

The game proceeds in this manner, with the leader then asking a question beginning with *wann*. For example:

Wann siehst du ihn (sie)?   When do you see him (her)?

The last questions asked by the leader are:

Was sagen die Leute von ihm?   What do people say about him?

Was sagt er dazu?   What does he say to that?

When all questions have been answered, everyone puts his piece of paper in a common pile or in a basket and draws another one out, with his eyes closed. When the resulting combinations of sentences are read aloud, they usually turn out to be quite humorous.

79. *Was tue ich?*   (What Am I Doing?)

AIM: To practice the imperative and the *du*-form of the verb in German sentences.

PLAYERS: The class is divided into two teams.

Each team makes a list of commands (each on a separate card) which a student can follow, such as:

Kämme dir die Haare!   Comb your hair.

Kaue Kaugummi!   Chew chewing gum.

Then, alternating between teams, a team member draws a command from the pile of commands written by the other team and does as the command instructs. If he cannot understand the instruction, his team forfeits a point and it is the other team's turn.

Students act out the command for members of their team, who may discuss in German what they think he is doing. But they may venture only two guesses, for example:

Du kämmst dir die Haare.   You are combing your hair.

Du kämmst dir die Perücke.   You are combing your wig.

If one of the two answers is correct, a team gets a point. If the grammar is also correct, the team wins an additional point. Then a member of the opposite team chooses a card and acts out the command for the members of his team.

80. *Setz dich!*   (Sit Down!)

AIM: To answer questions correctly in German.
PLAYERS: The whole class.

The whole class stands up and the teacher asks each student a question in German which he must answer correctly to remain standing. If a student makes a mistake, he must sit down and may not participate anymore. The last five people who remain standing score a point. Then everyone stands up again and the game continues.

   • As a variation, two teams can play, asking each other questions alternately. The team that lasts longer wins.

81. *Karte nach links*   (Card to the Left)

AIM: To answer questions correctly in German.
PLAYERS: The whole class.
NEEDED: A stack of cards with a question in German on each.

The class sits in a circle; the leader places a stack of cards with questions face down in front of him. The leader draws a card and reads the question aloud to his neighbor on the left. If his neighbor answers correctly, the neighbor gets to keep the card. If not, he takes the card from the leader and repeats the same question to his neighbor on the left. If his neighbor on the left answers the question correctly, he keeps the card.

   A card always moves to the left until it is answered correctly or returns to the leader. The player with the most cards at the end of the time limit wins the game.

82. *Fußball*   (Football)

AIM: To answer questions correctly in German.
PLAYERS: The class is divided into two teams.
NEEDED: A blackboard with a football field drawn on it.

The captain of one team asks the other team captain a question. If the captain asks the question incorrectly, or takes more than 30 seconds, or if the question isn't clear, his team gets a five-yard penalty. The captain of the other team has 30 seconds to answer the question. He may have all the help he needs from his players, but only he may give the answer. If the answer is reasonable and grammatically correct, his team advances ten yards and gets to answer another question.

If a team answers incorrectly, it loses the ball, which means that it must ask the other team a question, giving it a chance to advance ten yards.

Once a team scores a touchdown, it gets a chance for two extra points by answering another question.

A student may be chosen ahead of time to draw the football field on the blackboard and record the moves as each team advances the ball toward its goal (*Tor*). The team which scores the greatest number of touchdowns or has advanced farthest at the end of 20 minutes wins.

The team may wish to use the names of real German *Fußball* teams, such as *Berliner Fußballverein* or *Wiener Sparta*, but they should be reminded that *Fußball* (soccer), is quite different from football.

• The game may also be played by limiting the questions to a specific picture or topic.

83. *Fragen*   (Questions)

    AIM: To write questions about a given topic with emphasis on correct grammar.

    PLAYERS: The class is divided into two teams, one team to a row or table.

The teacher writes a word on the blackboard, for example, *die Familie*. Given a total of ten minutes, team members go to the blackboard, one at a time in order of the seating arrangement. Each player writes a sentence about the topic word, for example:

Wie viele Personen sind in deiner Familie?	How many people are there in your family?
Wer ist der älteste in deiner Familie?	Who is the oldest in your family?
Wie heissen deine Eltern?	What are your parents' names?

A space should be left under each question for writing the answer later in the game.

Teams compete simultaneously to construct correctly the greatest number of questions in German. Any errors in the sentence may be corrected only by the next person on the team, during his turn. Students may help each other as much as they like at their seats, but they forfeit a point if they help a person while he is at the board. After ten minutes, the teacher allots each team one point for every sentence it wrote correctly.

After the teacher has made the corrections, the teams have ten minutes to write the answers to the other team's questions in the space left below each question on the board. The procedure for answering is the same as for writing the questions, and points are scored in the same way.

Instead of setting a time limit, the teacher may call an end to the game when a team completes five questions, and may award that team an additional point for finishing first.

84. *Fragen, Fragen*   (Questions, Questions)

AIM: To ask and answer questions in German.
PLAYERS: The class is divided into two teams.

A player from one team asks a membre of the other team a question. If he makes a mistake in asking the question, his team loses a point. The team answering a question scores two points if its answer is reasonable and grammatically correct. Only one point is scored if an answer is grammatically poor or the pronunciation incorrect.

85. *Die kluge Flasche*   (The Intelligent Bottle)

AIM: To ask questions correctly in German.
PLAYERS: The whole class.
NEEDED: A bottle.

Students sit in a circle and a player asks a question that begins with the word *wer*, such as:
Wer wird am nächsten heiraten?   Who will marry next?

Then he spins the bottle, and the person to whom it points when it stops spinning is the answer to the question. This person asks the next question. Points are scored by students who make no errors in asking a question.

86. *Omas Küche* (Grandma's Kitchen)

AIM: To compose questions that start with *was* or with a *wo* compound and to answer the questions correctly in German.

PLAYERS: The whole class.

NEEDED: A box.

Each player writes a question that starts with *was* or a *wo* compound and drops it in a box. Examples of such questions are:

Womit spielst du?   What are you playing with?
Worauf sitzt du?   What are you sitting on?

A leader then goes to each player and asks him what he is giving Grandma for her kitchen. For example:

Leader:
Was gibst du Oma für die   What are you giving
Küche?   Grandma for her kitchen?

Player:
Ich gebe ein Messer.   I'm giving a knife.

A player may answer with any item, but no two students may name the same thing.

The leader goes around again, asking each player a question which he draws from the box. The player must answer with the object he has given Grandma for her kitchen. For example:

Ich sitze auf dem Messer.   I'm sitting on the knife.

If he laughs or smiles, he pays a forfeit. He may, for example, have to elaborate on his answer in German—to explain why he is sitting on the knife.

87. *Neun Vierecke*   (Nine Squares)

AIM: To comprehend the meaning of German phrases as quickly as possible and to facilitate thinking in German rather than translating English into German.

PLAYERS: The class is divided into two teams.

NEEDED: A blackboard with one large square divided into nine smaller squares. Each square should be at least 6 inches square and contain a prepositional phrase that begins with *in*. For example:

in dem Stall   in the stable

in dem Sack   in the sack

A flap of plain paper is taped over each square so that the phrase can't be seen, and the flaps are numbered, in horizontal order, from 1 to 9. On separate cards are phrases that begin with *wo* and match the nine phrases on the board. For example:

Wo das Pferd das Futter frißt.   Where the horse eats fodder.

Worin St. Nikolaus gute Sachen   Where St. Nicholas carries good
    trägt.   things.

Also needed are mimeographed sheets which duplicate the nine squares and the nine phrases on the board. The phrases should be planned so that no more than one prepositional phrase matches a phrase beginning with *wo*.

The leader passes out the mimeographed sheets face down. When everyone has a sheet, the leader tells the players to look at it for 60 seconds only and then put it away. When the 60 seconds are up, the leader draws a card and, alternating between teams, reads a phrase to a team member and asks him:

Welche Nummer?   Which number?

The team member then calls the number—in German—of the square where he recalls having seen the matching phrase. The leader then lifts the flap so that all can see the phrase in the square on the board. If there is a match, the team wins a point and the flap is torn off. The team with the greatest number of points when all of the nine squares on the board have been matched wins.

88. ***Bildertitel***   (Picture Title)

> AIM: To compose German titles for pictures.
> PLAYERS: The whole class.
> NEEDED: A picture cut from a magazine or newspaper for each
>   player. (If desired, all the pictures may be of one
>   kind, such as babies, animals, current news photos,
>   cartoons, etc.)

Each person is given a picture. Within a given time limit, he is to write a descriptive sentence or title for his picture in German. Students should try to be as imaginative and humorous as possible, and at the same time write accurate German. When the time is up, students display their pictures and read their captions. If desired, the group may vote on what it considers the best captions.

• As a variation, several student volunteers may prepare pictures for the group. The pictures are displayed in front of the group and each student is told to write a caption for each picture. The group or judges chosen from within it, can select the best caption for each picture from the various entries.

IX

Clue and Description Games

89. *Ich denke an 'was* (I Am Thinking of Something)

AIM: To identify an object by asking questions about its characteristics.

PLAYERS: The whole class.

A student comes to the front of the room, thinks of an object from the lesson, and says to the class:

Ich denke an 'was. I am thinking of something.

The student then calls on members of the class who have their hands raised, and they ask questions about the characteristics of the object. The person in front of the class answers in complete sentences. When someone thinks or knows what the object is, he indicates this by saying:

Ich weiss. I know.

The student in front of the room calls on him and says:

Schon gut, Klaus, was ist es? All right, Klaus, what is it?

If the player guesses correctly, he gets five points and takes the place of the person who was in front of the class. If he guesses incorrectly, he loses five points and the game proceeds until someone guesses correctly.

Once the object has been guessed, the game proceeds with a new object. It can also be played so that an answer is not accepted unless the article is correct.

54

90. *Ja oder Nein* (Yes or No)

AIM: To identify an object by asking questions about its characteristics.

PLAYERS: The whole class.

A person who is selected from the class thinks of an object (which the rest of the class knows how to say in German) and confides this word to the teacher. Students in the class then ask him questions about the object, to which he can reply only *ja* or *nein*, such as:

Ist es ein Tier?	Is it an animal?
Wohnt es in dieser Stadt?	Does it live in this city?
Ist es größer als ein Hund?	Is it bigger than a dog?

After 20 questions have been asked, each student writes down what he believes the object is.

One point is scored for a right answer. If the game is being played in teams, the team with the greatest number of correct answers wins. Then a new round is started as another student decides on an object and responds to questions about it with *ja* or *nein*.

• As a variation, students try to identify a famous personality, rather than an object, by asking 20 questions about him (or her) in German.

91. *Was ist es?* (What Is It?)

AIM: To identify an object by asking questions about its characteristics.

PLAYERS: The class is divided into two teams.

NEEDED: A pack of ten cards with a noun listed on each.

The pack of cards lies face down on a desk in front of the room. A student from Team One draws a card, reads it, and begins to give clues about the word to his team. His team also tries to find out as much as it can about the noun written on the card by asking questions. Once a team has ventured a guess about the object, its turn is up and the other team is permitted a guess. The team which guesses correctly scores a point. If neither team guesses correctly, no point is scored for that card. Teams alternate in drawing a card, and the game is over when all ten cards have been used.

• As a variation, teams can play simultaneously with separate packs of cards. For this version, it is best if the members of each team arrange their desks in a circle. Each pack of cards is placed face down on a player's desk and team members take turns drawing a card and defining the noun to their team-mates. The first team to guess all ten cards correctly wins. If English is spoken, or if there is any cheating (even pantomiming), the guilty team receives two new cards to define.

92. **Wer oder was bin ich?**   (Who or What Am I?)

AIM: To identify an object or name a person by asking questions about their characteristics.

PLAYERS: The class is divided into two teams.

NEEDED: A pack of cards with names of objects or people for each team.

The game is played like the preceding game, *Was ist es?* except that the person who gives the clues pretends to be the object or person on the card and gives them in the first person. For example:

Ich bin ein Filmstar.   I am a movie star.
Mein Haar ist lang and blond.   My hair is long and blond.

The person can be anyone who is known to everyone in the class, including students in the class.

Questions should be asked in the second person, such as:
Bist du Amerikanerin?   Are you an American?
Hast du einen Mann?   Do you have a husband?

The questions and answers should be in the form of complete sentences. The questioning continues until the object or the person's identity is learned. Then someone else selects a card and the game proceeds as before.

• As a variation, use cards with the names of jobs, instead of objects or people, and have the teams try to guess what the jobs are by asking questions in German.

93. ***X, Y oder Z?***   (X, Y, or Z?)

>   AIM: To determine which person experienced a certain
>   event by asking questions about it.
>   PLAYERS: The class is divided into two teams.
>   NEEDED: Three chairs in front of the class, marked *X*, *Y*, and *Z*.

Before the game starts, each student writes a short list of things he
has done in his life that most of his classmates probably don't know
about, such as a certain trip, an unusual experience, etc. The teacher
selects a list and calls three students from the class to sit in the
marked chairs in front of the room. He states the experience of one of
the panel members briefly to the class. For example:

>   *Er traf Bob Hope.*   He met Bob Hope.

The teacher should make sure that the statement applies to only one
of the three panel members.)

The students then direct questions to the panel members, X, Y,
and Z, about this experience. The following are sample questions:

>   *X, wie alt warst du?*   X, how old were you?
>   *Z, wo war es?*   Z, where was it?
>   *Y, war er freundlich zu dir?* Y, was he friendly to you?

In answering the questions each panel member tries to convince the
class that it was actually he who had the experience.

After ten minutes, the teacher asks:

>   *Wer tat es wirklich?*   Who really did it?
>   *War es X, Y oder Z?*   Was it X, Y, or Z?

Each team discusses (in German) which member of the panel it
thinks had the experience and writes either X, Y, or Z. When the
teams' guesses have been handed in to the teacher, she says:

>   *Ist die Person, die wirklich*   Is the person who really
>   *Bob Hope traf, X, Y oder Z?*   met Bob Hope X, Y, or Z?
>   *Bitte stehen Sie auf!*   Please stand up!

The person who actually had the experience stands up. A point is
awarded to each team which guessed correctly.

94. *Berühmte Personen*   (Famous People)

AIM: To identify a person by comprehending statements made about him in German.

PLAYERS: The class is divided into two teams.

NEEDED: Several biographical sketches of well-known personalties, living or dead. (Each sketch should consist of a number of fairly short sentences or clues and be arranged so that the person's identity becomes more obvious with each statement. Each sentence in the sketch should be numbered and the total number written at the top of the page.)

Teams take turns guessing the identity of the famous person as each statement about him is read aloud by the leader. If a member of either team guesses correctly after the first statement is read, his team receives as many points as there are statements in the sketch. As each statement is read, members of the two teams alternate in guessing, and a point is subtracted from the total score for the sketch for each ad ditional clue given. For example, if the sketch contains nine clues in all and a player guesses the personality correctly after the fourth clue is read, his team receives six points. No penalty is attached to a wrong guess; the biographical reading is merely continued until someone guesses the person's identity.

95. *Mein Geheimnis*   (My Secret)

AIM: To write several short descriptive sentences about an object with emphasis on the correct article and pronoun.

PLAYERS: Up to 30.

NEEDED: An 8 × 10-inch piece of cardboard or stiff paper for each player.

Each player writes on his cardboard the title *Mein Geheimnis* and lists a few clues below it. He shows his card to another player and reads the clues aloud. For example:

Mein Geheimnis	My Secret
Er ist klein.	It is small.
Er ist ein Tier.	It is an animal.
Er ist weiss.	It is white.
Er hat Katzen nicht gern.	It doesn't like cats.
Er ist klug.	It is smart.
Was ist er?	What is it?

(The pronoun should indicate the gender of the noun.)

Members of the group take turns guessing what the pronoun represents. The one who guesses the noun correctly and gives the correct article scores a point.

If the article is incorrect, the person with the secret says:

Artikel? Article?

The person who named the wrong article cannot receive the point, and the person with the secret calls on someone else to give the noun with the correct article, awarding him with a point if the answer is correct. The person awarded the point then takes his card with his *Geheimnis* and shows it to the group.

If one no guesses the secret of the first player, he turns the card over and shows the answer to the group—for example, *mein Hund* (my dog).

96. *Nein, nicht* (No, Not)

AIM: To ask questions about the characteristics of an object.

PLAYERS: Any number.

Players take turns asking a series of questions of the leader in an effort to ascertain the secret word. Each time the leader answers, he must name a proper noun in the category in question, in the following manner:

Ist es eine Stadt?	Is it a city?
Nein, es ist nicht Neu York.	No, it is not New York.
Ist es ein Film?	Is it a film?
Nein, es ist nicht The Graduate	No, it is not *The Graduate.*
Ist es ein Mann?	Is it a man?
Ja, aber is es ist nicht Beethoven.	Yes, but it isn't Beethoven.

If the secret word has not been guessed after 20 questions, the leader reveals it. If a player guesses the secret word, he becomes the leader for the next round. Otherwise, a new leader is chosen by the students.

97. *Baseball*

AIM: To define words in German with emphasis on correct grammar.

PLAYERS: The class is divided into two teams.

NEEDED: A stack of cards with a German word to define on each card.

Each team must first decide on a batting order. The first player on the team at bat draws a word to define, and advances one base for each correct definition he gives. After he has given three definitions, his team tries to guess the word. If the team guesses correctly, the player scores a home run and the next player on the team comes to bat. If a player makes a mistake, he's out. If a player gets to third base but his team does not guess the word correctly, he remains on third base and can advance to home only if a teammate gets to third base. After three outs, the next team gets its turn at bat.

98. *Hast du es gern?*   (Do You Like It?)

AIM: To give clues to an object in German with emphasis on the phrase *gern haben*.

PLAYERS: Ten or more.

A player goes out of the room while the others choose a word or object. The player returns and tries to guess the word or object by asking each player, in turn, how he likes it and listening carefully to the answers. For example:

Wie hast du es gern?	How do you like it?
Ich habe es gern mit Pfeffer.	I like it with pepper.
Ich habe es gern heiss.	I like it hot.

If he can't guess from the answers, he asks:

Wann hast du es gern?	When do you like it?
Wo hast du es gern?	Where do you like it?

The player from whom he gets the last clue takes his place.

99. *Was fehlt in dem Kuchen?* (What's Missing in the Cake?)

AIM: To describe words related to a given category.
PLAYERS: About ten.
NEEDED: A large spoon, a bowl, and a sign for each player (except the *Koch* [cook]) that shows a picture of a particular ingredient for a cake. Under the picture is the name in German, for example, a picture of two eggs and the words *zwei Eier*.

The players form a circle. In the center is the *Koch*, blindfolded, who pretends to be vigorously stirring cake batter in a bowl with a large spoon. The players in the circle stand around him and say:
Etwas fehlt in dem Kuchen.   Something's missing in the cake.
The *Koch* points to someone in the circle and asks what is missing. The person describes the ingredient he represents in German.
Koch:
Was fehlt in dem Kuchen?   What's missing in the cake?
Player:
Sie sind rund und weiss.   They are round and white.
In der Mitte sind sie gelb.   They are yellow in the middle.
When the *Koch* has guessed the ingredient, the player joins the *Koch* in the circle and is blindfolded. Then both say in unison: *Was fehlt in dem Kuchen?* The blindfolded *Koch* again indicates someone in the circle, and the player shows his picture and replies. Blindfolded players may help the *Koch* guess. The game continues until all the ingredients have been added to the cake.
   • As a variation, the game can be called *Was fehlt in dem Wohnzimmer*, or *Was fehlt in der Schule?* etc., with the players representing items related to the title.

100. *Was man nicht sagt* (What Someone Doesn't Say)

AIM: To give clues to words within a name.
PLAYERS: The class is divided into two teams.
NEEDED: A pack of cards containing names of famous people.

Teams take turns drawing a card from a deck of cards that is lying face down. After drawing a card, a player gives clues to words contained within the name he has drawn by having team members guess the words he leaves out of a sentence. For example, if a card says "Elizabeth Taylor," the clues might be:

Ein Herr, der einen Anzug macht heisst auf englisch ein	A man who makes a suit is called a .... in English.
Der zwölfte Buchstabe des Alphabets ist	The twelfth letter of the alphabet is ....
Das Englische für "ist" ist	The English for *ist* is ....
Man schläft auf einem	A person sleeps on a ....

(Answers: Tailor, *L*, is, *Bett*)

101. *Hinky Pinky*

AIM: To give clues to words in German.
PLAYERS: The class is divided into two teams.

Each team sits in a circle and the teams play simultaneously. A player on one of the teams starts by giving clues to a "Hinky Pinky" which he has thought of. A Hinky Pinky is a combination of two words, one German and one English, which rhyme—as follows:

blau cow, *heiß* nice, *gut* boot, *Bett* get, etc.

The person describes his Hinky Pinky without giving the equivalent of either of the words in German or English and without pantomiming. Clues for the Hinky Pinky "*blau* cow" might be:

Das erste Wort ist auf deutsch.	The first word is German.
Die Farbe des Himmels.	The color of the sky.
Zweites Wort: ein Tier.	The second word: an animal.
Man ißt gern sein Fleisch.	People like to eat its meat.
Es gibt Milch.	It gives milk.

When the team has guessed it, the Hinky Pinky is recorded and the next person on the team gives clues to his Hinky Pinky. The team that has guessed the greatest number of Hinky Pinkies after 20 minutes wins.

102. *Was sagst du?* (What Do You Say?)

AIM: To guess what object a student represents by descriptions in German of his reactions to a given set of conditions.

PLAYERS: The class is divided into two teams.

Each team chooses a student to sit on a panel in front of the class. The teacher then assigns each member of the panel the object he must represent. One of the teams starts the game by setting a scene for the members of the panel, as in the following example:

Das Wetter ist sehr schlecht.	The weather is very bad.
Es regnet und blitzt.	It is raining and lightning.
Was sagst du?	What do you say?

Then each member of the panel answers as if he were the object assigned to him.

Panel members, if assigned the word for tree and cat, might answer as follows:

Der Baum:	The Tree:
Ich verliere meine Blätter.	I'm losing my leaves.
Ich habe Angst vor dem Blitz.	I'm afraid of the lightning.
Aber ich brauche das Wasser vom Regen.	But I need the water from the rain.
Die Katze:	The Cat:
Mein Pelz wird so nass.	My fur is getting so wet.
Ich hasse den Ragen mehr als den Hund.	I hate the rain more than I hate dogs.

When both panel members have responded, the other team sets the scene and the panel members respond to it. Then each team is permitted one guess as to the identity of the object its panel member represents. If a team guesses incorrectly, the other team is allowed one guess. A correct guess is worth five points. Then each panel member selects a person from his team to take his place and a new round of the game commences.

The game may be modified by showing the teams four words, two of which represent the objects assigned to the panel members. And Sometimes the two panel members might have the same assignment. If the words or objects are difficult, the teams might set a third and a fourth scene to which the panel members can respond.

103. *Gegensätze*   (Contrasts)

AIM: To practice composing descriptive sentences with emphasis on adjectives.

PLAYERS: The class is divided into two teams.

A player of the first team forms a descriptive sentence with a predicate adjective, such as:

Karl ist jung.   Karl is young.

A player on the other team replies as quickly as possible with a contrasting descriptive sentence. He should use a contrasting adjective in the predicate when possible, such as:

Karl ist alt.   Karl is old.

The second player, if he has formed a contrast correctly, recites another descriptive sentence, for which the first team must supply a contrast. The teams continue alternating in this way.

Each team tries to answer quickly and accurately. If a player's response is not correct, another member of the same team may try, until a correct sentence has been given. A new sentence can be introduced only by a player who has responded correctly to the previous sentence. The teacher acts as moderator, deciding whether a player has answered correctly, before the game may continue.

A point may be awarded to a team that presents a sentence accurately on the first attempt.

104. *Der Dieb*   (The Thief)

AIM: To identify a player with an object by asking questions about it.

PLAYERS: The class is divided into two teams.

NEEDED: A classroom or school auditorium (even a shopping center can be used).

Each team is divided into two equal halves, one of which is called *die Diebe* and the other *die Detektive* (the detectives). Each thief writes a note telling where he's going and proceeds to that place, where he "steals" an item. Five minutes later a detective from the opposing team discovers the thief's note and follows him to the designated place. He finds the thief there and a dialogue such as the following commences:

Detektiv:	Detective:
Aha, Dieb, gefangen!	Aha, thief, you're caught!
Was du gestohlen hast,	I can guess what you've
kann ich raten.	stolen.
Dieb:	Thief:
Raten mal,	Guess, if you can.
wenn du kannst.	I am a thief, but
Ich bin Dieb, aber	no liar.
kein Lügner.	

The detective then questions the thief to find out what he has taken. The thief must answer correctly, with *ja* or *nein*, to every question, but need not give any other clues.

All students return to a central meeting place at a specified time, and the team with the greatest number of detectives who have identified all of the "stolen" items wins.

105. *Wo ist die Büroklammer?* (Where Is the Paper Clip?)

AIM: To practice describing locations in German.
PLAYERS: The class is divided into two teams.
NEEDED: A paper clip or other small object.

One player is sent from the room, an object is hidden by the other team, and the player returns. The leader of his team then asks him:

Wo ist die Büroklammer?   Where is the paper clip?

The player guesses:

Sie ist auf dem Tisch.	It is on the table.
Sie ist in dem Umschlag.	It is in the envelope.

His teammates answer *nein*—unless, of course, he has guessed where it is.

The player may walk to a different spot in the room after each guess. If he has moved closer to the object, students answer in a loud voice. But the player may not move until he has guessed (in German) where the paper clip is.

A team acquires a point for each time one of its members asks a question. At the end of the game, the team with the least amount of points is the winner.

106. *Die Statuen* (The Statues)

AIM: To describe locations with emphasis on correct grammar.

PLAYERS: Up to 40.

NEEDED: A variety of objects familiar to the group.

The players line up in two teams and each player holds an object in his hand. Each team then chooses one of its members to be the *Statue,* who stands a short distance from his team. At a signal from the leader, the first player on one team runs to the *Statue* and arranges him in the position desired—as a scout gazing into the distance, a dancer in a pose, etc. The first player then holds up his object, gives the German word for it, and places it somewhere about the *Statue*— in his hand, on his head, on the ground, etc. The *Statue* must correctly identify the location of the object within three tries to score a point for his team. And the grammar must be correct.

He may state, for example:

Der Stein ist auf dem Baden   The stone is on the ground
  zwischen den Beinen.   between my legs.

Then a player from the other team takes a turn and does likewise with his team's *Statue.* He may put a hat on the head of the *Statue* or a bunch of flowers in his hand, in an effort to make the *Statue* look funny, but he also must name the object in German. The game continues with the teams taking turns.

At each turn, the person on the team that last placed an object on or near the *Statue* becomes the new *Statue.* A leader keeps score and announces the winning team. The game can be hilarious.

107. *Sätze* (Sentences)

AIM: To practice writing descriptive sentences with emphasis on correct grammar.

PLAYERS: The class is divided into two teams.

NEEDED: A blackboard and chalk.

Each team is assigned a word, such as *der Festzug* (parade) or *der Herbst* (fall), and both teams play simultaneously. The student who sits in the first seat in the first row goes to the blackboard and writes a descriptive sentence about the word. If he makes errors in his sentence, only the next person in his row is permitted to correct them, when it is his turn to go to the board. Students may help each other as much as they like when everyone is seated, but they forfeit a point if they help a person while he's at the board. The game is over when a row completes its seventh sentence.

The row which finished first scores a point for winning the race. Each row also scores a point for each sentence which is grammatically correct.

108. *Welches Bild ist meins?*   (Which Picture Is Mine?)

AIM: To describe pictures in German.
PLAYERS: The whole class.

Students draw a quick sketch using subjects whose names are familiar to them in German. Then each student composes five sentences that contain clues for describing his picture. The teacher collects the pictures, chooses five of them, numbers them and, puts them in front of the class. Then the teacher calls on one of the sketchers to describe his picture (with or without notes), as follows:

Hans, beschreibe dein   Hans, describe your
  Bild, bitte!   picture, please.

After giving five clues, the student asks:

Welches Bild ist meins?   Which picture is mine?

Students write down the name of the artist and the number of the picture he has just described. Each person who has guessed correctly receives a point for that picture.

109. *Grosses Bild*   (Big Picture)

AIM: To describe a picture with emphasis on correct grammar.
PLAYERS: The class is divided into two teams.
NEEDED: A blackboard and chalk.

The teams go to the board and together they draw a composite picture using objects whose names are familiar to them in German.

At the end of the time limit, the students go back to their respective teams. Alternating between teams, students write or recite a descriptive sentence about the "big picture." A team gets two points if its sentence is perfectly correct, and only one point if there is an error in grammar or pronunciation.

The descriptive sentences can be limited to emphasize a particular grammatical concept, such as prepositional phrases that tell "where", the use of nouns in the plural, and so on.

110. *Der verrückte Künstler*   (The Crazy Artist)

AIM: To describe an unusual picture clearly enough so that others can draw one like it.
PLAYERS: The whole class.

Each student draws an imaginary object (an apple with four legs and one big eye at its stem, etc.), signs the picture, and gives it to the teacher. The teacher selects a picture and calls on the artist who drew it (*der Künstler*) to describe it to the rest of the students in the class. Without looking at the picture, students listen to his description and try to draw an identical picture. They may ask *der Künstler* questions in German if they wish.

After the artist has finished describing his picture, he draws it on the board so that the students can compare their copies with the original drawing he described to them. Students then discuss in German the quality of his description, and award him from one to five points accordingly. (A vote may be taken.)

• As a variation, and instead of a "crazy" picture, students could be asked to draw a landscape, an indoor picture, an action picture, or the like.

111. *Kleider*   (Clothing)

AIM: To describe how persons should wear certain clothes.
PLAYERS: The class is divided into two teams.
NEEDED: Two bags of clothing (clothing and parts of clothing can be labeled).

Each team takes a bag of clothes and describes how each member of the opposing team should wear certain articles of the clothing. After 20 minutes, teams exchange the bags and the descriptions as to how the apparel should be worn. (The teacher may want to check the descriptions for correct grammar.) Each team then has ten minutes to dress as directed in the accompanying descriptions. After ten minutes, the team which is dressed more closely in keeping with the descriptions wins.

112. *Die Kopie* (The Copy)

AIM: To give and to follow directions for the placement of objects.

PLAYERS: The class is divided into two teams.

NEEDED: Two bags of objects whose German names are familiar to the class and two small tables, one in the front and the other in the back of the room.

Each team assigns half of its members to be the builders (*Bauer*) and the other half to be the observers (*Aufseher*). The builders from each team take a bag and begin setting its items on a table as the observers from the opposing team look on. After five minutes, the builders draw a diagram of the arrangement of the items on a piece of paper. The observers approve the drawing and keep it.

When both teams of observers have received the completed diagram, the builders put the objects back in the sack, put the sack on the table, and join the observers from their own team in front of the opponents' table. Using the diagram (but not permitting the builders to look at it), the observers must explain the former arrangement of the items to the builders on their team. The builders try to duplicate the arrangement, based on the description. After 15 minutes, the team whose arrangement of items most closely resembles the original arrangement—as illustrated in the diagram—wins.

113. *Scharaden*   (Charades)

AIM: To determine, in German, what a person is trying to pantomime.

PLAYERS: The class is divided into two teams.

NEEDED: A prepared list of famous people, song-titles, book titles, names of movies, etc., arranged by categories, and each title or name on a separate slip of paper. Also, a stop watch or a watch with a second hand.

Each team member must act out a charade before the rest of his own team, who must try to guess what he is portraying before three minutes have elapsed. The leader sits in a central place, holding a box containing the slips of paper and a watch. The first player on the first team comes up and draws a slip from the box. He must then announce what category he is performing. For example:

  Der Titel eines Buches.   The title of a book.

The leader begins the timing, and the players on the first team try to guess what he is doing. If they fail to guess within three minutes, he must reveal the name to them, and they get no score. If they succeed, the leader notes the elapsed time. Then the first player on the second team takes a turn; and the teams continue to alternate in this manner until all players have acted out a charade. The team with the shorter total time and the fewer misses is the winner.

114. *Was machen wir?*   (What Are We Doing?)

AIM: To determine, in German, the action or event a group is pantomiming.

PLAYERS: Any number, divided into several small groups.

One group secretly decides on an action which they will pantomime in a comical manner. Then they say to the rest of the group:

  Was machen wir?   What are we doing?

The group may pantomime that they are en route to Mars, scientists in the Antarctic, football players, employees held up by a bank robber, etc. The more ridiculous the pantomime, the more fun the game is. The others try to guess. If their guesses are partially right, the group encourages them.

  Then the group explains what it has been doing and another group takes a turn.

X

Map Games

115. *Stadt, Land, Fluss*   (City, Country, River)

AIM: To become acquainted with a map of Europe.

PLAYERS: The whole class.

NEEDED: A map of Europe large enough for everyone to see,
          or separate maps for each student to work with.

Everyone sets two sheets of paper next to each other and writes
geographical categories across the top. Then a letter of the alphabet
is chosen and everyone tries to write a German word beginning with
the prescribed letter to fit each category. A student's entries might
look as follows:

	Stadt	*Land*	*Fluss*	*Gebirge*
E	*Essen*	*England*	*Elbe*	*Erzgebirge*

When the first person has finished, everyone must stop and draw
an "X" under any category which is left blank. Then another letter
is chosen and the game continues. At the end, everyone adds up his
entries and the person with the most wins.

• As a variation, use categories other than those related to
geography.

71

116. *Städtenennen*   (Naming Cities)

AIM: To name German cities.

PLAYERS: The whole class.

NEEDED: A map of Germany for each student or a map large enough for all to see.

Beforehand, the teacher prints a different letter of the alphabet on separate pieces of paper. A student draws a piece of paper and announces the letter to the class. Everyone then has five minutes to make a list of German cities that begin with this letter. At the end of five minutes, someone reads his list aloud, and all the cities which he has listed must be struck out on the other students' sheets. Often the students that had the biggest lists to begin with end up with most of the cities crossed out. The person who has the most cities at the end of the game wins, and he draws a new letter of the alphabet.

117. *Stadtnamen*   (Names of Cities)

AIM: To locate German cities on a map.

PLAYERS: The class is divided into two teams.

NEEDED: A large map of Germany.

The first player on Team One locates a city on the map, points to it, and asks:

Warum reist du nach Bonn?   Why are you traveling to Bonn?
The first palyer on Team Two responds by naming the city mentioned and saying that he intends to buy something there. The purchase must begin with the same letter as the city. For example:

Ich reise nach Bonn,   I am going to Bonn
  um ein Buch zu kaufen.   to buy a book.

If he does this correctly, he wins a point for his team. Then he must locate another city and direct the same kind of question to the next player on Team One.

118. ***Die Post***   (The Mail)

AIM: To become acquainted with the names of German cities.

PLAYERS: Ten to 20.

NEEDED: A list of cities, various pieces of "mail" in a bag, and a chair for every player except one.

One player is assigned to be *der Briefträger* (Mailman), and each of the other players is given the name of a city by the leader. Then the players place their chairs in a circle and sit down, except for the *Briefträger*, who stands in the center. Beside him on the floor is a bag that represents a mailbag. The *Briefträger* reaches into this bag, brings out a piece of mail (for example, a newspaper), and says the following (using the name of the city that is on the piece of mail):

Ich habe eine Zeitung   I have a newspaper
von München, die   from Munich, which is
nach Bonn geht.   going to Bonn.

The two players who were assigned the names of these two cities jump up and try to exchange places—as the *Briefträger* also dashes over and attempts to sit on one of the chairs. The student who is unsuccessful in occupying a chair becomes the next *Briefträger*. He goes to the center of the circle, reaches into the mailbag, and brings out another piece of mail, which he assigns to two cities in the same manner as before. The procedure is repeated with each exchange.

119. ***Eine Reise***   (A Trip)

AIM: To locate German cities on a map.

PLAYERS: The class is divided into two teams.

NEEDED: Two large maps of Germany and a card or paper for each player on which are written the names of two German cities (such as *Bonn – München* or *Frankfurt – Hamburg*.

The cards are placed face down, one on each player's desk. Both teams play simultaneously, and the players on each team take turns.

A player turns his card over, goes to his team's map, and draws a line connecting his two cities as quickly as he can. He calls out the names as he does so, winning a point for his team if he draws the line correctly. If he cannot find the cities on the map within a set time, his team does not score a point. In either case, he returns to his seat and the next player on his team takes his place at the map.

The game is over when one of the teams has used up all its cards. Each team then counts the number of points it has received for the cities it has correctly located, and the team which finished first receives an additional five points. The team with the largest total of points wins.

• As a variation, the game can be played in the same manner with large maps of Europe and cards which have the names of cities in all countries where German is spoken.

120. *Ein Landkartenspiel*   (A Map Game)

AIM: To associate languages with the countries in which they are spoken and to locate these countries on a world map.

PLAYERS: The class is divided into two teams.

NEEDED: A map of the world large enough for everyone in the class to see and a list of languages (in German).

Each team designates one of its members "the Professor," and the Professor from each team stands before a map of the world while the team members look on. A player from Team One asks where a particular language is spoken, whereupon the professor from Team Two answers the question in German and points to the country where the language is spoken.

Player, Team One.
Wo spricht man Deutsch?   Where is German spoken?
Professor, Team Two:
Hier spricht man Deutsch,   German is spoken here [pointing
in Deutschland.   to the map] in Germany.

To win a point for his team, a Professor must answer his questioner correctly in German and locate the country on the map within 30 seconds. If he cannot do so, his team forfeits a point and someone else from his team takes his place as the new Professor. Then a player from Team Two directs a question to Team One's Professor, and the game continues in this manner until one of the teams scores ten points.

121. ***Nullen und Kreuze*** (Zeros and Crosses)

AIM: To answer questions about the culture of Germany.
PLAYERS: The class is divided into two teams.
NEEDED: A blackboard with a blank tic-tac-toe diagram.

Each team chooses a captain. Although the team members may contribute any piece of information to their captains, only the captain is permitted to give the final answer for his team. The game starts with the teacher directing a question (such as the following) to the captain of Team One:

Wo ist der Schwarzwald? Where is the Black Forest?

The captain may obtain help from his teammates in answering the question; however he has only 30 seconds to answer. Assume he answers:

Der Schwarzwald ist in The Black Forest is in
Norddeutschland. northern Germany.

The captain of Team Two considers the answer carefully, and then responds by saying *wahr* if he feels the question was answered correctly and *falsch* if he thinks the answer was incorrect. The teacher then gives the correct answer to the question:

Der Schwarzwald ist in The Black Forest is
Süddeutschland. in southern Germany.

If Team Two indicates that it knows the correct answer, it has a chance to enter its mark on the tic-tac-toe board. (One team's mark is a zero [*Null*] and the other team's mark is a cross [*Kreuz*].) In this example, since Team One's answer to the question was false, Team Two must answer *falsch* to win the opportunity of placing its mark on the tic-tac-toe board.

The first team to score a tic-tac-toe wins the game.

XI

Song Games

122. *Drei Worte singen* (Singing Three Words)

AIM: To add to a German song in groups of three words.
PLAYERS: The class is divided into two teams.

To begin, all players are standing, and someone from Team One sings the first three words of a song. Someone from Team Two then sings the next three words—no more and no less—and the singing alternates between the teams so that every student gets a chance to contribute. When someone cannot contribute, or makes a mistake, he must sit down, and he will not have another chance to contribute to the song. When this happens, the next person on the opposing team takes his turn. If he also makes a mistake, both teams stand again and the game continues with a new song.

Each time a player sings the next three words correctly, he scores a point for his team. Every time a new song is started, it marks the beginning of a new round, and all the players must stand. The game is an incentive for students to memorize songs thoroughly.

• As a variation, choose a song that everyone in the class knows well and in every line delete the last syllable, then the last two syllables, and so on, so that each line becomes shorter.

• Another variation is to have one team sing a line, the next team the next line, etc. However, all nouns must be deleted from each line so that there is a pause in the melody at these points. Allowing for the pauses makes it difficult to pick up the melody again and the effects are quite comical.

123. **Wort im Lied**   (Word in Song)

> AIM: To use a German word in the context of a German song.
> PLAYERS: The class is divided into two teams.

Each team selects nouns or verbs from German songs which the class has been practicing. A player from Team One names one of the words which his team has selected. The opposing team then has 20 seconds to recall the word in its setting; that is, to repeat the word in a verse where it appears. More than one verse may be applicable, but any verse which contains the word is acceptable. For example: *Wie treu sind deine Blätter* is a response to the word *Blätter*. A team scores by responding correctly within the allotted time.

124. **Liederklopfen**   (Song Tapping)

> AIM: To identify a German song by its rhythm rather than by its words or melody.
> PLAYERS: The class is divided into two teams.

Because every song has a rhythm of its own, a member of one team taps out the rhythm of a German song without giving any clue to the melody. To win a point, the other team must guess correctly which song it is supposed to be.

125. **Liedertitel**   (Song Titles)

> AIM: To translate song titles.
> PLAYERS: The class is divided into two teams.
> NEEDED: Cards on which are written the titles of German songs.

Each team forms a row and the leader hands the first player in one of the rows a card with a song title on it. The player must read the title aloud and then give a correct English translation of it. If his answer is correct—with allowance made for a fairly free translation—he scores one point for his team. He then goes to the back of his row and the first player in the other line gets a card. The procedure is repeated, and the game continues until all the players have had one turn or until all the cards have been used.

Below are some song titles that may be used. Of course, others may be added.

Ach, wie ist's möglich denn?	"Oh, How Then Is It Possible?"
Annchen von Tharau	"Annil from Tharau"
Du, du liegst mir im Herzen	"You, You Are in My Heart."
Guten Abend, gute Nacht	"Good Evening, Good Night"
Herzlich tut mich erfreuen	"I Really Like It"
Ich hatt' einen Kameraden	"I Had a Friend"
In einem kühlen Grunde	"In a Cool Glen"
Kein Feuer, keine Kohle	"No Fire, No Coal"
Kommt ein Vogel geflogen	"A Bird Came Flying"
O Tannenbaum, O Tannenbaum	"Oh Christmas Tree, Oh Christmas Tree"
Sah ein Knab' ein Röslein steh'n	"A Boy Saw a Little Rose"
Spinn, spinn, meine liebe Tochter	"Spin, Spin, My Dear Daughter"
Stille Nacht, heilige Nacht	"Silent Night, Holy Night"
Suse, liebe Suse	"Susy, Dear Susy"
Wenn die Soldaten durch die Stadt marschieren	"When the Soldiers March through the City"
Wenn ich ein Voglein wär"	"If I Were a Little Bird"

XII

STORYTELLING GAMES

126. *Der Schnurball*   (The Ball of String)

AIM: To tell a story in round-robin form.
PLAYERS: The class or a small group.
NEEDED: A ball of string marked off at different segments or
          lengths. Different colored string tied together in
          varying lengths could also be used.

A student starts by telling a story in German as he slowly unwinds
the ball of string. When he comes to the end of the first segment, he
hands the ball of string to someone else who must continue the story
as he slowly unwinds the second segment of string. The game continues until everyone has contributed to the story or until the ball of
string is fully unwound.

127. *Geschichte aus dem Sack*   (Story out of a Sack)

AIM: To build a story around specific objects.
PLAYERS: The class or a small group.
NEEDED: A bag or container and miscellaneous items.

A student begins by drawing an object from a bag filled with various
items and building a story around it, Then he passes the sack to
someone else in the class, who draws another object out of it and
continues the story by incorporating the new object in the ongoing
story line.

79

128. *Geschichte durch Bilder*   (Story through Pictures)

AIM: To build a story around pictures.
PLAYERS: The class or a small group.
NEEDED: A stack of pictures from magazines and a watch with
          a second hand.

A student starts the game by selecting a picture at random and building a story around it. After 30 seconds, another person draws (or is
given) a picture and continues the story, incorporating his picture
into the context. After 30 seconds, the next person selects another
picture and continues the story in the same manner, and so on.

129. *Eine ABC Geschichte*   (An ABC Story)

AIM: To tell a story with restrictions on the first letter of
          each noun.
PLAYERS: The class or a small group.

It is fun and also challenging to write or tell a story in which each
noun begins with the next letter of the alphabet. A noun which does
not fit the sequence of the alphabet cannot be used, and every noun
must make sense in the context of the story. "Q", "X," and "Y" can
be left out.

130. *Komische Geschichte*   (Funny Story)

AIM: To tell a story that uses many adjectives.
PLAYERS: The class or a small group.

Each person has two pieces of paper. On the first piece he writes a
short story in which he uses 12 adjectives. Instead of writing the
adjectives, however, he merely designates their places in the story
with a short line.

On the second piece of paper he writes the 12 adjectives one under
the other, leaving off the adjective endings for example, *gross*, *blau*,
heiß, etc. Then each person gives this list of adjectives to his neighbor
on the right to use in completing his story.

Each person then reads his own story, but substitutes for the blank lines of his story the adjectives given him in the order they appear on the paper.

For example, a story may begin as follows:

Ein ————— Hase lief durch einen ————— Wald.

Spät am ————— Abend sass er hinter einem —————

Busch, etc.

The first four words on the list he receives may be *grun, nass, niedlich,* and *achteckig.*

A person scores a point for each adjective he includes with the correct grammatical ending. If he also corrects a misused article in so doing, he receives two additional points.

NTC GERMAN MATERIALS

Computer Software
Basic Vocabulary Builder on Computer

Graded Readers and Audiocassettes
Lustige Dialoge, *Walbruck*
Lustige Geschichten, *Walbruck & Henschel*
Spannende Geschichten, *Walbruck*

Graded Workbooks
Aufsätze mit Bildern
German Verb Drills
Jetzt schreiben wir, *E. Hugo*
Wir können doch schreiben, *E. Hugo*

Text and Audiocassette Package
Just Listen 'n Learn German

Cross-Cultural Awareness
Im Brennpunkt: Deutschland
Briefe aus Deutschland, *R. Leyding*
The Magazine (duplicating masters),
  A. Culver
Unterredungen aus Deutschland,
  G. Dekovic; ed., M. Lazar
Kulturelle Begegnungen, *R. Shirer*
Briefe über den Ozean, *H. Walbruck*
Amerikaner aus Deutschland, *Walbruck*
Everyday Conversations in German,
  G. Cumming
Let's Learn about Germany

Jochen und seine Bande Series
Abenteuer in Hinterwalden
Mit Thespis zum Süden

Comic Mysteries, *H. Wolff*
Die Jagd nach dem Familienerbe
Das Geheimnis im Elbtunnel
Hoch in den Alpen
Innsbrucker Skiabenteuer

Plays and Comedies
Zwei Komödien, *G. A. von Ihering*
Ein Hotel namens Europa,
  G. A. von Ihering
Gehen wir zum Theater!, *E. Konig*

Wir sprechen Deutsch Series, *H. Walbruck*
Deutschland — einmal anders
Deutschland — einst und jetzt
Ich bin ein Berliner
Ich bin ein Hamburger
München — heimliche Hauptstadt
Deutsche Volksfeste
Besuch im Schweizer Mittelwesten

Legends and Fairy Tales
Von Helden und Schelmen
  aus deutschen Sagen, *K. Reiter*
Von Weisen und Narren
  aus deutschen Märchen, *K. Reiter*
Das Max und Moritz Buch, *W. Meier*

Duplicating Masters
Lotto: German Vocabulary Bingo, *J. Olsen*
Lotto: German Verb Bingo, *J. Olsen*
Das Kreuzworträtselbuch, *S. Ehrlich*
Das Rätselheft, *S. Ehrlich*
The Magazine, *A. Culver*
The Vocabulary Builder, *D. Liebowitz*

Grammar References
Guide To German Idioms
German Verbs and Essentials
  of Grammar
Nice 'n Easy German Grammar
German Verbs and Essentials of Grammar

Bilingual Dictionaries
Klett's Modern German/English Dictionary
Klett's Super-Mini German/English Dictionary
The New Schöffler-Weis: German/English
  Dictionary
Harrap's Concise German and English Dictionary
German Picture Dictionary

For further information or a current catalog, write:
National Textbook Company
a division of *NTC Publishing Group*
4255 West Touhy Avenue
Lincolnwood, Illinois 60646-1975 U.S.A.